3

MODERN WAYS
WITH TRADITIONAL
SCOTTISH RECIPES

To My Family
The best "test panel" of all

Modern Ways With

TRADITIONAL SCOTTISH RECIPES

Rosalie Gow

PELICAN PUBLISHING COMPANY
GRETNA 1981

Copyright © 1980
By Rosalie Gow
All rights reserved
First published in the United Kingdom in l980
by The Ramsay Head Press

Pelican Edition
First printing, October 1981

Library of Congress Cataloging in Publication Data

Gow, Rosalie.
  Modern ways with traditional Scottish recipes.

  Includes index.
  1. Cookery, Scottish.   I. Title.
TX717.3.G68   1981   641.59411   81-15756
ISBN 0-88289-304-1   AACR2

Manufactured in the United States of America

Published by Pelican Publishing Company, Inc.
1101 Monroe Street, Gretna, Louisiana   70053

Contents

Introduction

New ways with Traditional Scottish Recipes is a light-hearted but practical blend of new and traditional Scots cooking, designed to appeal to native Scots as well as to visitors to the Scottish scene.

Recipes are for the best, the simplest and the most delicious eating that Scotland has to offer and include such diverse delights as "Cloutie Dumpling" and "Drambuie Soufflé", "Crofter's Porridge" and "Smoked Salmon Roulades". All the recipes have been completely modernised but old methods remain undisturbed wherever necessary—e.g. The Haggis has been de-frocked but "Jugged Hare" remains in all its original glory. Each recipe is shown in Imperial, Metric and American measurements and serves 4 people, unless otherwise indicated.

The line drawings are by Maureen Mooney.

MEASUREMENTS

Metric and American conversions are shown to the nearest, practical equivalent and are therefore not mathematically exact. (For example, a French housewife would probably buy ½ kg of meat rather than 450 g, although the latter is the closer equivalent to 1 lb.) *It is, however, important to use (a) all Imperial (b) all Metric or (c) all American measurements in any one recipe and not to mix them.*

WEIGHTS FOR SOLID MEASUREMENTS

British Imperial and American	Metric	Notes
Ounces	*Approx. No. of Grams*	*Notes*
½ oz	15 g	1. *Measurements given in tablespoon* equal *level* tbsps unless otherwise stated and are virtually the same in British, Metric or American measurements.
1 oz	25 g	
2 oz	50 g	
3 oz	75 g	
3½ oz	100 g	
4 oz (¼ lb)	125 g	One 5 millilitre spoon = 1 tsp or American measuring tsp.
5 oz	150 g	
6 oz	175 g	
7 oz	200 g	One 15 millilitre spoon = 1 tbsp or American measuring tbsp.
8 oz (½ lb)	225 g	
9 oz	250 g	
10 oz	275 g	2. Where self-raising flour is used in British recipes, add baking powder to plain flour in the proportion of ½ level tsp (5 ml spoon) to 4 oz (125 g or one American measuring cup.)
11 oz	300 g	
12 oz (¾ lb)	350 g	
13 oz	375 g	
14 oz	400 g	
15 oz	425 g	
16 oz (1 lb)	450 g	
2.2 lbs	1 kilogram (kg)	

American Measurements	*Approx. no. of Ounces*	*Approx. Metric Grams*
1 measuring cup (8 fl oz capacity)		
Butter and Fats	8 oz	225 g
Breadcrumbs, soft	2 oz	50 g
Cheese, grated	4 oz	125 g
Dried Fruit	5-6 oz	150 g

American Measurements	Approx. no. of Ounces	Approx. Metric Grams
Flour (see note 2 above)	4 oz	125 g
Rice (dry)	8 oz	225 g
Nuts, chopped	4 oz	125 g
Suet, shredded	4 oz	125 g
Sugar, granulated or caster	8 oz	225 g
icing (confectioner's)	6 oz	175 g
soft brown or demerara	8 oz	225 g
Syrup	11½ oz	315 g

LIQUIDS

British Imperial (Fluid Oz)	Approx. Metric millilitres	Approx. American
1	25 ml	2 tbsps
2	50 ml	¼ cup
4	125 ml	½ cup
5 (¼ pint)	150 ml	10 tbsps
6	175 ml	¾ cup
8	225 ml	1 cup
10 (½ pint)	275 ml	1¼ cups
12	350 ml	1½ cups
15 (¾ pint)	425 ml	1¾ cups + 2 tbsps
16	450 ml	2 cups (1 pint)
20 (1 pint)	575 ml	2½ cups
30 (1½ pints)	850 ml	3¾ cups
35	1 litre	4¼ cups + 2 tbsps
40 (2 pints)	1.150 litres	5 cups
60 (3 pints)	1.705 litres	7½ cups

Note British Imperial Pint = 20 fl oz (1 quart = 40 fl oz)
American Pint = 16 fl oz (1 quart = 32 fl oz)

OVEN TEMPERATURES

Oven	°F	°C	Gas
Low	200	100	Low
Cool	225-250	110-130	¼-½
Very Slow	250-275	130-140	½-1
Slow	275-300	140-150	1-2
Very Moderate	300-325	150-170	2-3
Moderate	350-375	180-190	4-5
Moderately Hot	400	200	6
Hot	425-450	220-230	7-8
Very Hot	475-500	240-260	9-10

Soups
and Starters

CULLEN SKINK

This tasty soup is made with smoked fish—the recipe is adapted from a very old traditional Scots dish.

Ingredients	Imperial	Metric	American
2 smoked filleted haddocks (usually sold as "yellow fillets")	about ½ lb	225 gms	½ lb
Milk	½ pint	275 ml	1¼ cups
3 good sized potatoes, thinly sliced			
1 onion, finely chopped			
Water	1½ pints	850 ml	3¾ cups
Salt and pepper to taste			
2 tbsps cream (optional) and small pat butter to garnish—finely chopped parsley (optional)			

Place filleted fish and milk in a saucepan and bring very slowly to just under boiling point. Cook very gently until fish becomes opaque. Flake fish, cover and set aside.

In another pan, cook potatoes and onion in the water until tender, then rub through a wire sieve or mouli mill. Combine with fish and milk and season to taste. Add cream, if used, and butter.

Garnish with parsley before serving.

COCK-A-LEEKIE

Old, traditional recipes suggest adding a dozen or so "unbroken prunes" to this soup, half an hour or so before serving—I have never had the courage to do this but YOU can, if you like!

Serves 6-8

Place an old cock or fowl (or chicken) in a large pan and nearly cover it with cold water. Add 1 tbsp (1-15 ml spoon = 1 tbsp) salt, 12 peppercorns, 4-6 parsley stalks, 1 small bay leaf, small sprig of thyme (optional) and a small, quartered onion. Bring to the boil, skim, then cover and simmer until the bird is tender, turning it once or twice. The giblets can be added to the pot but not the liver. Simmering time will be roughly 2 hours; remove bird, strain soup and return it to the washed pan. To the soup now add the whites of 6 leeks, cut into 1" lengths and shredded, and 2 rounded tbsps of rice. Simmer until leeks are tender, adjust seasoning.

A little chopped meat from the bird can be added to the soup, the remainder of the meat being served separately, e.g. with caper sauce.

LENTIL SOUP

Serves 4-6

Ingredients	Imperial	Metric	American
Streaky bacon (or a ham bone or bacon end)	2 oz	50 gms	2 oz
Cold water	about 2 pints	1¼ litres	5 cups
Lentils	3 oz	75 gms	¼ cup
1 onion, peeled and quartered			
1 large carrot, peeled and quartered			
Small piece of turnip			
Salt and pepper			

Cut rind from bacon and put both bacon and rind, together with all remaining ingredients except seasoning, into a large saucepan. Bring slowly to the boil and simmer for at least one hour. Remove bacon rind or ham bone but leave in the meat. Put the soup, including bacon and vegetables, through a mouli mill or coarse sieve, or blend for a few seconds in an electric liquidiser. Return soup to the pan, reheat and season to taste. Garnish—serve with cubes of fried bread or sprinkle with a little dried mint.

PARTAN BREE

Serves 4-6

("Partan" = Crab and "Bree" = Soup). A centuries-old recipe.

Remove the meat from one large, boiled crab, keeping the claw meat separate. Place 4 oz (125 ml—½ cup) long grain rice in a pan with 1 pint (575 ml—2½ cups) milk and bring to the boil. Stir in ¼ tsp salt, cover and simmer gently for about 20 minutes until rice is soft. Stir in crabmeat (reserving claw meat). Purée in an electric blender or by pressing through a sieve. Return to the pan. Stir in 1 pint (575 ml—2½ cups) light stock and bring back to the boil. Add claw meat and adjust seasoning. Remove from heat. Stir in ¼ pint (150 ml—12 tbsps) light cream and dust with paprika before serving.

11

SCOTCH BROTH

Many Scots still talk of "eating" their soup rather than drinking it and, with good, thick broth such as this, one can see why. It pays to make a fairly large quantity of broth at one time, even for a family of four, as this soup tastes even better the second day.

Serves 8-10

Ingredients	Imperial	Metric	American
Stock, made from mutton or beef bones (or you can use 3 stock cubes)	3 pints	1¾ litres	7½ cups
¼ teacup lentils			
¼ teacup barley			
Salt to taste—coarse cooking salt for preference			
¼ teacup whole peas (if you use dried peas soak them overnight)			
2 large onions, peeled and coarsely grated or chopped small			
1 medium onion, peeled and coarsely grated or chopped small			
Small piece of turnip, peeled and coarsely grated or chopped small			
2 large leeks, chopped fine			
A few small leaves of kale, if available, chopped fine			
Half of a small cabbage (do NOT chop)			
Pepper			

If you are using meat bones to make the stock, place them in 3 pints (1¾ litres—7½ cups) of cold water, along with the lentils and barley; bring to the boil, cover and simmer gently for an hour; remove the bones, add salt to taste (you will need very little if using stock cubes) and sufficient water to make the stock up to its original level. Add the remaining vegetables, bring back to the boil and simmer for another half an hour. Remove the cabbage and discard it; adjust seasoning to taste.

One of the most interesting shops in Orkney (you cannot miss the Royal Coat of Arms above its door) is Scott's Fish Shop, in Bridge Street, just opposite Kirkwall harbour. The Royal Warrant, I was intrigued to discover, was granted for supplying not fish but cheese (home-made on a farm at Dounby and "discovered" by the Duke of Edinburgh) to the Queen Mother. Scott's are justly famed for their special cure—a closely guarded secret which took seven years to perfect—for the most succulent smoked salmon and sea trout ever tasted. It is now exported all over the world—to Canada, China, Johannesburg and Vienna—even behind the Iron Curtain and to the "adjacent island of Great Britain". Scott's will export in small quantities (sides from 2½ to 3 lbs) to individual customers or smoke your own salmon for you, if you are lucky enough to catch one, receiving and despatching it by air or 1st class mail. Mrs Watson, the owner, showed me how she cut the salmon obliquely, from tail to head, in thin slices which she first brushed with olive oil. All it then needed, before serving, was a liberal sprinkling of fresh lemon juice and some brown bread and butter to go with it but I also used it in a smoked salmon cocktail (recipe below) which we enjoyed as a luxury starter to a self-catering holiday supper one night.

√ORKNEY SMOKED SALMON COCKTAIL

Serves 2

Ingredients	*Imperial*	*Metric*	*American*
Thinly sliced smoked salmon, cut into strips about 1" x ½" (2½ x 1¼ cms)	**2 oz**	**50 gms**	**2 oz**
2 small firm tomatoes, skinned and roughly chopped			
Cocktail Sauce:			
Thick Mayonnaise	**3 tbsps**	**3 x 15 ml spoons**	**3 tbsps**
Juice from jar of pickled onions	**1 tsp**	**1 x 5 ml spoon**	**1 tsp**
Good squeeze lemon juice			
Tomato Purée	**1 level tsp**	**1 x 5 ml spoon**	**1 tsp**
Horseradish sauce (optional)	**1 level tsp**	**1 x 5 ml spoon**	**1 tsp**
2-5 drops Tabasco			
Shredded lettuce heart			
Lemon wedges			

Prepare salmon and tomatoes. Blend sauce ingredients and fold in salmon and tomatoes. Line two glasses with shredded lettuce and pile cocktail mixture in the centre. Spear a wedge of fresh lemon onto the rim of each glass.

KIPPER PATÉ

Frozen kippers save tiresome boning in this inexpensive and piquant paté

Serves 6

Cook 8 oz (225g = 8 oz) frozen kipper fillets according to package instructions. Discard the skin. Pound the flesh with a wooden spoon until as smooth as possible. Blend in 2 oz (50g—¼ cup) softened butter, ½ small clove crushed garlic (optional), a good dash of freshly ground black pepper and 1 tsp (1 x 5 ml spoon = 1 tsp) strained lemon juice. Turn into a small serving dish (preferably a straight sided earthenware one), pat well down and smooth over the top.

Serve as a first course or snack with either melba toast or thinly sliced brown bread and butter. Or use for cocktail canapes—spread on tiny squares of toast and garnish with parsley or small pieces of black olives.

CROWDIE OLIVES

You can't make too many of these for any party—they look intriguing and taste even better. (If you cannot buy Crowdie, which is made in Scotland, sieved cottage cheese may be substituted).

Makes 32

Ingredients	Imperial	Metric	American
Pkt Philadelphia cream cheese	3 oz	75 gms	3 oz
Carton Crowdie cheese	5 oz	150 gms	5 oz
Hazelnuts or walnuts, chopped	2 oz	50gms	½ cup
16 pimento-stuffed green olives			

Beat cheeses together to blend thoroughly. Chop nuts finely. Roll a stuffed olive in the centre of a heaped teaspoonful or so of cheese, then toss in finely chopped nuts, to coat.

Chill for at least an hour. Cut in halves, crosswise, before serving.

SCOTCH SEAFOOD COCKTAIL

Choose a variety of fresh cooked or smoked seafood—e.g. mussels (smoked mussels are available in bottles and are a good choice), crabmeat or shrimp, some smoked and flaked smokie, and some thin strips of smoked salmon. Fold into the same cocktail sauce as used in "Orkney Smoked Salmon Cocktail" and serve with lemon wedges, on a bed of lettuce hearts.

SMOKED ROE PATÉ

Ingredients	Imperial	Metric	American
Smoked cod's roe (can be bought in jars when not otherwise available)	8 oz	225 gms	8 oz
1 clove garlic, skinned and crushed to a paste with ¼ tsp salt			
1 shallot or small onion, grated			
Lemon juice	about 1 tbsp	1 x 15 ml spoon	1 tbsp
Tabasco, or freshly ground black pepper to taste			
Fresh white breadcrumbs (soak in half its volume of cold water, then squeeze dry)	2 oz	50 gms	1 cup
Olive Oil	about 1 tbsp	1 x 15 ml spoon	1 tbsp

Skin roe, if necessary. Pound in a mixing bowl with remaining ingredients, adding enough olive oil to make a smooth paste. Pack into jars, smooth top and chill. (Will keep for a week, kept chilled).

SALMON AND SHRIMP PATÉ

Ingredients	Imperial	Metric	American
Cooked salmon and/or shrimps (fresh, tinned or frozen)	8 oz	225 gms	8 oz
Softened fresh butter	2 oz	50 gms	¼ cup
Lemon juice, tabasco and salt to taste			
Clarified butter (i.e. gently melted then skimmed or strained to remove the "froth")	1 tbsp	1 x 15 ml spoon	1 tbsp

Drain fish, if necessary. Pound ingredients together; pack into small dishes when as smooth as possible. Level the top and seal over with clarified butter. Keep chilled and eat within a week.

SMOKED SALMON ROULADES

This is an expensive and exceptional delicacy, to be served on very special occasions for very special guests.

Serves 8

Ingredients	Imperial	Metric	American
Cooked smoked trout (fresh or tinned)	4 oz	125 gms	4 oz
Well softened butter	1 oz	25 gms	⅛ cup
Very thick double cream	4 tbsps	4 x 15 ml spoons	4 tbsps
Thick mayonnaise	1 tbsp	1 x 15 ml spoon	1 tbsp
Finely chopped fresh herbs, parsley alone will do, parsley and chervil together, for preference	1 level tsp	1 x 5 ml spoon	1 tsp
Salt and tabasco to taste			
Squeeze of lemon juice			
8 postcard size pieces of thinly sliced smoked salmon (you will need three 3 oz packages), or approximately	8 oz	225 gms	8 oz
Aspic glaze—aspic jelly powder, lemon juice, tabasco			

If smoked trout is fresh, pre-cook by poaching lightly in water, white wine and lemon juice, plus salt, 4 peppercorns, 3 or 4 parsley stems and a strip of thinly pared lemon rind. Skin, bone and flake the fish, when cool. Blend and pound filling ingredients together until they form a thick, creamy paste. Divide into 8 portions, having carefully adjusted the seasoning, and place each portion in the centre of a piece of smoked salmon. Roll up neatly, tucking in the ends, and place in a row on an oblong serving dish.

To make aspic glaze, dissolve a ½ pint (275 ml—1¼ cup size) package of aspic jelly powder in ¼ pint (150 ml—10 tbsps) liquid, made from strained juice of 1 lemon + hot water. Season with a few drops of tabasco, to taste, and cool by stirring over ice. When aspic thickens and is about to set, brush it over roulades to coat each well. Allow remaining jelly to set in a container— before serving, chop roughly and spoon round the roulades on their serving dish. Each of the roulades can be decorated with a tiny cress leaf or sliver of truffle and re-glazed, if you wish.

SMOKED SALMON STARTER

Serve thinly sliced smoked salmon (1-2 small slices) with lettuce, fresh lemon wedges, thinly sliced and buttered brown bread. Black pepper corns in a pepper-grinder are an essential accompaniment.

Fish Dishes

FISH

Nowhere in the world is there better fish—or a greater variety of fish—to be found than in Scotland and great trouble is taken to see that it arrives fresh to as many homes as possible. The "Fish-Man's" van is a welcome sight on city streets and country roads, once and often twice a week. There are many different kinds of smoked fish to be enjoyed in Scotland too, from the exclusive salmon to the humbler herring—although the latter is a splendid fish and cheap only because, until very recently when the herring shoals have diminished alarmingly because of over-fishing, it has always been so plentiful. And no visitor to Scotland should think of leaving without having tried a brown-skinned, creamy fleshed Arbroath Smokie.

ARGYLL MACKEREL

So called because I learned how to cook them like this—fresh caught and in the open air—on a fishing holiday in Argyll.

"Group some large stones together on the beach in a rough circle and build a fire in the small centre space. Heap seaweed on top and lay the cleaned, sea-rinsed mackerel on the seaweed to cook".

In the absence of beach and seaweed, the following more orthodox recipe is very good! Be sure that the mackerel are really fresh (stiff and shiny with bright, protruding eyes) as they go off more quickly than other fish.

Ingredients	*Imperial*	*Metric*	*American*
4 fresh mackerel			
Salt and pepper			
A little mild, prepared mustard			
Butter, melted	1 oz	25 gms	2 tbsps

Wash and clean the mackerel and remove the heads. Sprinkle inside with salt and pepper. Close up the fish in their original shape and make four cross-wise slashes, almost through to the bone, on each. Spread mustard lightly inside the slashes. Brush over with melted butter and place on foil under a hot grill until thoroughly cooked through, turning once.

Serve at once, with brown bread and butter and a tomato salad.

ARBROATH SMOKIES

Smokies are fresh haddocks which have been cleaned, cured and smoked whole (not flattened out, like smoked "kippered" herrings) and are usually bought in pairs, tied together at the tails with (smoked!) string. They are already cooked and virtually require only to be heated through in some way. They can be steamed in a shallow pan of hot water or wrapped in foil and

18

heated through in a moderate oven. To serve, gently flatten out the fish (skin side down) and remove the backbone—it comes away very easily. Add a pat of butter and some freshly ground pepper. Serve with hot buttered toast for breakfast, tea or supper.

Variations

Many delicious things can be done with smokies. A lightly poached egg is sometimes set on top of the hot, buttered smokie and the flaked flesh is also excellent in an omelette, in kedgeree with hard boiled egg, or folded into a thick white sauce and used to fill vol-au-vent cases.

COD'S ROE

In season during February and March, you can buy cod's roe raw, boiled or smoked. The boiled roe needs only to be sliced about ½″ (1½ cm) thick and fried in butter—served with fried potatoes and fresh tomatoes, it makes an appetising main course. Raw fish roe must first be boiled in salted water for 30-40 minutes, depending on thickness, then allowed to cool before frying.

FISH, LEEK AND POTATO PIE

A good "one-dish" meal which I like to serve with the pickled beetroot I feel goes so well with fish.

Serves 4

Ingredients	Imperial	Metric	American
4 good sized leeks			
Filleted whiting or other white fish	**¾ lb**	**350 gms**	**¾ lb**
4 thin strips lemon peel, parsley stalks, pepper, salt, water			
Butter	**1½ oz**	**40 gms**	**3 tbsps**
Flour	**1½ oz**	**40 gms**	**3 tbsps**
Milk			
Boiled mashed potatoes	**1½ lbs**	**675 gms**	**1½ lbs**

Trim most of the green part of the leeks away. (They can be used in soup.) Split and wash the whites and place with fish in a saucepan. Just cover with water and add lemon peel, parsley, pepper and salt. Simmer until fish becomes opaque. Drain stock into a bowl, removing peel and parsley. Make up to ½ pint (275 ml—1¼ cups) with creamy milk. Place fish in a buttered dish with the leeks.

Melt butter in another pan and stir in the flour, without letting it brown. Gradually stir in stock from the fish plus milk and bring to the boil. Season and pour over fish. Top with mashed potatoes and brown in a hot oven.

19

FINNAN HADDIE AND RICE CASSEROLE

"Finnan Haddie" is paler than other smoked haddock and split but not filleted before curing.

Serves 4-6

Lay 1 lb (450 g — 1 lb) finnan haddie (smoked haddock), filleted and skinned, in a buttered dish. Season with pepper—no salt. Beat 3 egg yolks and mix with ½ pint milk (275 ml—1¼ cups) and pour this over the fish. Sprinkle on evenly 6 oz (175 g—¾ cup) uncooked long-grain rice. Cover the dish with a lid or kitchen foil and bake in a moderate oven (375°F/190°C—mark 5) for about 45 minutes or until rice is tender and has absorbed all the liquid. Dot with butter and sprinkle sparingly with salt. Place 2-3 sliced tomatoes round the edge of the dish and return it to the oven for 10 minutes.

STUFFED BAKED HERRINGS

Fine fresh herrings and an unusual savoury stuffing make this inexpensive lunch or suppertime dish a treat.

For the stuffing, peel and grate 1 large cooking apple and 1 small onion. Combine with 3 oz (75 g—1½ cups) soft, white breadcrumbs, chopped parsley, salt and pepper to taste, and bind with 1 small beaten egg. Use to stuff 4 large, filleted herrings and fold each fish over into its natural shape. Place fish in a greased oven dish, cover with a lid or kitchen foil and bake in a pre-heated, moderate oven (375°F/190°C—mark 5) for 15 minutes. Uncover the dish, dot fish with a little butter and return the dish to the oven (uncovered) for a further 10 minutes or until herrings are cooked through and browned on top.

Serve hot, with pickled beets or a cabbage salad and brown bread and butter.

HERRINGS IN OATMEAL "wi' a delicate air"

Split filleted herrings in two lengthwise. Starting at the tail end, carefully strip off the skin. Dip each piece of fish first into lightly beaten egg white (it should be frothy but not stiff) and then into fine-ground oatmeal. Fry in butter in a shallow pan, turning once, when medium brown.

Serve with bread and butter. I like to accompany these herrings with a mustardy mayonnaise, mixing about ½ tsp (½ x 5 ml spoon—½ tsp) mild, made mustard with 1 tbsp (1 x 15 ml spoon—1 tbsp) thick mayonnaise.

PICKLED HERRINGS

Takes at least 2 days to "pickle". Serve as a starter course, or as part of a cold buffet.

Serves 6

Ingredients	Imperial	Metric	American
6 filleted herrings, fresh or salted			
Black pepper			
1 medium onion, thinly sliced			
2 small bay leaves			
Mustard seed	¼ level tsp	¼ x 5 ml spoon	¼ tsp
3-4 dried chillies			
Vinegar and water	Approx ¼ pint each	150 ml each	10 tbsps each

Sprinkle the rinsed herrings with pepper and, if unsalted, with salt. Put into a dish, in layers, with the onion, bay leaves, mustard seed and chillies. Cover with the vinegar and water and store for 2 days or longer in a cool place or refrigerator.

Remove from pickle before serving and garnish the plate with lettuce and lemon.

SOUSED HERRINGS

Prepare and sprinkle fresh herrings with salt and pepper as above, then roll up with the skin on the outside. Place close together, so that the fish cannot unroll, in an oven dish, adding 6-8 cloves. Pour in vinegar and water (or the liquid from a jar of pickles or pickled onions, does well) to come half way up the fish. Cover dish with foil or a lid and bake in a very moderate oven (325°F/170°C—mark 3) until fish is opaque—about 25 minutes. Allow to cool in the liquid and serve cold, with salad.

"Wha'll buy caller herrin',
They're bonnie fish and halesome farin',
Buy my caller herrin',
New drawn frae the Forth . . . ."

From the song "Caller Herrin'" by Baroness Nairne, words by Nathaniel Gow.

21

GRILLED MACKEREL WITH GOOSEBERRY SAUCE

A sharp, tangy sauce is the perfect compliment for this naturally oily fish, rich in flavour as well as protein.

Make the sauce first as the fish should be served straight from the grill. Top and tail ½ lb (225 g—½ lb) green gooseberries, place them in a small pan. Just cover the berries with cold water and add 1 oz (25 g—2 tbsps) sugar. Bring to the boil and simmer until tender, then press through a fine sieve. (When fresh green gooseberries are out of season, simply purée bottled or tinned berries, omitting extra sugar and water.)

Wash, clean and remove the heads from 4 fresh mackerel. Sprinkle the insides with salt, pepper and a little lemon juice. Close up the fish and make four crosswise slashes, almost through to the bone, on each. Brush with melted butter and place under a hot grill until thoroughly cooked through, turning them once. Bring to the table very hot, garnished with lemon and parsley. Serve gooseberry sauce separately.

KIPPERS

Kippers are herrings which have been split open and flattened before curing and smoking. The finest kippers are said to come from Loch Fyne—these are paler and less "red" than other kippers and certainly very good although I personally have tasted none finer than the Orkney-cured kippers I enjoyed there.

Buy the largest, thickest kippers you can—half of a juicy, fat kipper is much better fare than a whole, thin one. A good sized kipper contains enough natural fat to cook in its own juice and you cannot do better than simply grill it, skin upwards, under a hot grill. To serve, turn the fish flesh side upmost and add a knob of butter. (Cooking time approx. 5 minutes.)

SALMON MOUSSE

An easy main course for entertaining, especially as it doesn't mind being kept waiting.

Serves 6-8

Ingredients	Imperial	Metric	American
Tinned pink salmon (or 1 lb fresh salmon, poached as fish in previous recipes)	**14-16 oz**	**400-450 gms**	**2 x 7 oz cans**
Softened butter	**3 oz**	**75 gms**	**⅜ cup**
Salt and pepper			
Double cream	**¼ pint**	**150 ml**	**10 tbsps**
Thick mayonnaise	**2 tbsps**	**2 x 15 ml spoons**	**2 tbsps**

Ingredients	Imperial	Metric	American
Gelatin	**1 oz** **(2 envelopes)**	**2 x 15 ml spoons**	**2 tbsps**
Cold water	**6 tbsps**	**75 ml**	**6 tbsps**
Chicken stock (1 cube) or strained liquid in which fresh salmon was cooked	**¾ pint**	**425 ml**	**1¾ cups + 2 tbsps**
2 egg whites			

To decorate—cucumber, lettuce, lemon wedges, 8 whole cooked prawns (optional).

Drain salmon and remove any skin and bone. Using a fork, mash with butter in a bowl and season well. Whisk cream until thick but not stiff and fold into salmon, with mayonnaise. Sprinkle gelatin over cold water in a cup, place cup in hot water and stir until gelatin has dissolved. Stir into chicken stock and cool until syrupy—rather like raw egg white. Blend with salmon mixture, then gently fold in stiffly beaten egg whites. Turn into a 6″ (approx. 15 cms) souffle dish (or use an oiled cake tin and unmould before serving) and leave to set for several hours or overnight.

Garnish with thin, overlapping slices of cucumber round the outside edge. Place mousse in the centre of a large, round plate. Around the mousse arrange lettuce leaves, lemon wedges and the prawns, if used.

SMOKED FISH PATTIES

Serves 4-6 (makes 12 small patties)

Ingredients	Imperial	Metric	American
Smoked filleted haddock (sometimes called "yellow fillets")	**4-6 oz**	**125/175 gms**	**4-6 oz**
2 hard boiled eggs			
Mayonnaise	**1 tbsp**	**1 x 15 ml spoon**	**1 tbsp**
Salt and pepper			
Finely chopped parsley	**2 tbsps**	**2 x 15 ml spoons**	**2 tbsps**
Pastry:			
Self-raising flour	**8 oz**	**225 gms**	**2 cups**
Pinch salt			
Lard	**4 oz**	**125 gms**	**½ cup**
1 egg, beaten			
1 tsp vinegar			

Steam the fish until opaque, on a plate over a saucepan of boiling water. Leave fish to cool. In a bowl, mash hard-boiled eggs with mayonnaise, salt and pepper and chopped parsley.

For the pastry, sift flour and salt together and rub in the lard. Reserve 1 tbsp beaten egg to glaze tops, switch remainder with vinegar and fork into the flour mixture. Add a little cold water if necessary to make a firm dough. Roll out on a floured surface and cut into circles in two sizes, using pastry cutters approx. 3¼" and 2¾" (8½ x 7 cm) to line 12 buttered patty tins (with the larger circles) and make lids (with the smaller circles).

Flake the cooled fish and combine with the egg mixture. Spoon into lined patty tins. Brush pastry lids with cold water and put in place, moist side down. Press edges to seal. Brush tops with reserved egg. Cut two small slits in each patty and bake in a hot oven (425°F/220°C—mark 7) until golden brown— 18 to 20 minutes.

Serve hot with carrots and parsley sauce, or cold with potato salad and celery.

SMOKED HADDOCK AND CHEESE SAVOURY

This is made from "Golden Fillets"—filleted haddock which has been smoked an almost-orange colour—and is one of the tastiest savouries I know. It never fails to win acclaim when produced for a "company" lunch and is a family favourite too.

Serves 4-6

Ingredients	Imperial	Metric	American
Golden fish fillets	1 lb	450 gms	1 lb
Milk	1 pint	575 ml	2½ cups
Butter	2½ oz	65 gms	5 tbsps
1 medium onion, chopped			
4 rashers lean bacon, quartered			
4 tomatoes			
Flour	1½ oz	40 gms	4 tbsps
Pepper (no salt)			
Grated cheese	2 oz	50 gms	½ cup

Cover fish with milk and bring slowly to the boil in a covered pan. Simmer gently for 10 minutes or until fish is opaque. Meanwhile, melt 1 oz (25 g—2 tbsps) of the butter and gently fry the onion and bacon together for 5 minutes. Pop tomatoes into boiling hot water for 2 minutes so that skins will peel off easily, then chop. Make a cheese sauce by melting the remaining 1½ oz (40g—3 tbsps) butter and stirring in the flour, then gradually adding the milk in which the fish was cooked. Use only medium heat and stir throughout. Season with pepper only as the fish is already quite salty. Stir in cheese.

Finally place a layer of fish (as unbroken as possible) in a buttered dish, cover with onion, bacon and tomato, then another layer of fish. Pour cheese sauce over all. Place dish near the top of a hot oven (425°F/220°C — mark 7) until bubbly and speckled with brown.

Serve with creamed potatoes or rice or brown bread and butter.

THATCHED COD OR HADDOCK
My own favourite white-fish dish.

Ingredients	Imperial	Metric	American
4 fairly thick pieces of filleted cod or haddock			
Lemon juice			
Butter	**2 oz**	**50 gms**	**½ cup**
"Thatch"			
1 small onion, chopped			
1 tomato, chopped			
Soft white breadcrumbs	**4 oz**	**125 gms**	**2 cups**
Salt, pepper, chopped parsley and thyme			

Line a baking tin with foil and place fish on it in a single layer. Sprinkle with lemon juice and spoon on about a quarter of the melted butter. Soften the onion and tomato in the remaining butter and mix with crumbs, seasoning, etc. Arrange over fish and bake in a moderately hot oven (400°F/200°C — mark 6) for 20 minutes.

SMOKED SALMON QUICHE
For a party buffet or starter course to Christmas dinner.

Ingredients	Imperial	Metric	American
Shortcrust pastry	**8 oz**	**225 gms**	**8 oz**
Thinly sliced smoked salmon, cut into small pieces about 1" square	**4 oz**	**125 gms**	**4 oz**
4 eggs, mixed with creamy milk or single cream	**½ pint**	**275 ml**	**1¼ cups**
Finely grated cheese	**2 oz**	**50 gms**	**¼ cup**
Finely chopped onion, fried gently until softened in butter	**2 tbsps**	**2 x 15 ml**	**2 tbsps**
	½ oz	**15 gms**	**1 tbsp**
Salt and pepper			

Roll out the pastry on a floured surface and use to line an 8" fluted china flan dish or an 8" (20 cms) flan ring set on a baking tray—in the latter case, butter the ring and tray.

Distribute the smoked salmon and softened onion over the base of the pastry case, gently pour in beaten eggs and cream, then sprinkle evenly with grated cheese. Sprinkle with salt and pepper.

Bake in a moderate oven (375°F/190°C — mark 5) for about 35 minutes or until filling is risen, golden brown and just firm to the touch. This can be served either hot or cold—we like it better hot and it can be made in advance (deep-frozen, if you wish) and re-heated gently.

TROUT "ALMONDINE"

This makes a perfect luncheon party dish and is simplicity itself to make.

Wash and clean 4 small river trout but leave them whole. Dip them in 2 oz (50 g — 6 tbsps) flour, seasoned with salt and pepper. Heat 2 oz (50 g — 2 tbsps) butter and 2 tbsps (2 x 15 ml spoons — 2 tbsps) oil in a large frying pan and fry the trout gently, turning them once, until golden brown. Remove fish to a heated serving dish and keep warm. Brown 2 oz (50 g — ½ cup) blanched slivered almonds in the frying pan, add a good squeeze of lemon juice. Empty contents of frying pan over the trout. Serve with sauté potatoes and a green salad.

To cook for large numbers

The trout are easily "oven-fried"—place them in a foil lined baking tin, in single layer, having sprinkled inside the fish with salt and pepper. Drizzle with melted butter and lemon juice. Cook near the top of a hot oven (425°F/220°C — mark 6-7) until flesh of the fish is opaque—roughly 20 minutes. Flaked almonds can be browned in the same tin—be sure to run the lemon/buttery juices from the pan over the fish, when serving.

POACHED SALMON OR TROUT

This is the best method of cooking, if you are going to eat the fish cold, with salad. Fish should NEVER be boiled!

Cradle the fish in a strip of cheese-cloth or muslin, so that it can be easily lifted out when cooked. Quantities for cooking about 2½ lbs (1¼ kg) of fish are approx.—

    1½ pints (850 ml — 3¾ cups) cold water + ¼ pint (125 ml — 10 tbsps) white wine or wine vinegar
    ½ level tsp (½ x 5 ml spoon — ½ tsp) salt, 12 peppercorns
    Juice of ½ lemon + thin strip lemon peel, without pith
    1 large sprig parsley, with the stalks, which have the most flavour
Lower the fish into this, bring slowly to just under boiling point and simmer very gently—the water should be just visibly moving—until the fish is opaque and not a minute longer—roughly 20 minutes. Let cool in the liquid.

TO COOK FRESH TROUT

Unless the fish has been filleted for you, simply clean it out, leaving on the head and tail and without flattening the fish. Line grill pan with foil, having removed the rack. Place fish on the foil, sprinkle with salt, pepper and lemon juice and drizzle with some melted butter. Cook under a medium-hot grill until flesh is opaque—no longer—turning fish only once, if it is being cooked whole. Do not turn filleted fish at all.

If you do not have a grill, fry gently in butter, adding seasoning and a good squeeze of lemon to the dripping in the pan. Pour pan juices over the fish, when serving.

Brown or rainbow trout is very good too if coated with oatmeal before frying. In this case, I prefer to fillet the fish, and pat the oatmeal (medium ground is best but any kind will do) into the skinned flesh—I feel it is wasted on the skin, which I don't like to eat anyway. This way, you have the full benefit and flavour of the crisp coating of oatmeal next to the flesh. Serve with lemon wedges and parsley.

GRILLED SALMON STEAKS

Allow one steak, ½" to ¾" (1¼ cm to 2 cm) thick, per person. Grill as in "To Cook Fresh Trout" recipe, allowing approximately 5 minutes on each side.

Garnish with lemon and parsley sprigs and, at the last moment before serving, top each steak with a pat of lemon or anchovy butter.

Lemon or Anchovy Butter—

Make this ahead of time and chill. Soften about ½ oz (15 g — 1 tbsp) butter per serving. With the flat of a broad knife, blend in some finely chopped parsley and either as much lemon juice as the butter will absorb or 1 tinned anchovy fillet (drained and pounded to a paste) per ounce of butter. Form into little pats, about ¼" (½ cm) thick and 1" (2½ cms) in diameter and score the tops with a fork. Lay pats in single layer on a flat plate and chill until required.

Meat Dishes

"Some hae meat that canna eat,
And some wad eat that want it,
But we hae meat, and we can eat,
And sae the Lord be thankit...."

> The Covenanters' Grace—
> (Repeated by Robert Burns when dining with
> the Earl of Selkirk and often also called "The
> Selkirk Grace").

MINCE AND TATTIES

"Mince" is perhaps the most basic of all Scottish meat dishes—and there are many, many variations of it. It can be stewed, baked or even boiled (I do not recommend the latter), thickened with flour, breadcrumbs, oatmeal or barley—seasoned as you will and served with boiled or mashed potatoes, or with triangular "snippets" of toast. It can be brown, savoury and delicious—or an uninteresting grey, watery mess. Here is my basic version.

Ingredients	Imperial	Metric	American
Fat or oil (beef dripping, for preference) approx.	**1 oz**	**25 g**	**2 tbsps**
1 large onion, chopped			
Minced beef steak (which should include a small amount of fat)	**1 lb**	**450 g**	**1 lb**
About 1 level tsp salt and freshly ground pepper, to taste			
A handful (about 1 rounded tbsp) of oatmeal or porridge oats			
Half a teacupful water or stock from the boiling potatoes			

Melt the fat in a thick saucepan and, when sizzling, put in the onion, then the beef and brown quickly, stirring to prevent sticking. Add seasoning and oatmeal. Stir in water or stock and simmer for 20 minutes—some cooks stew mince for an hour or more but this, in my view, is very much to its detriment.

Serve with boiled or mashed potatoes.

N.B. Although not strictly speaking "Scottish", you can add vegetables to the mince and I particularly like fresh green peas cooked in the same pan; all three of my children insist on having baked beans stirred into the mince (almost blasphemous) so we often compromise by adding both peas AND beans and by cooking my grandmother's favourite "doughballs" on top!

DOUGHBALLS

Mix together 4 oz (125 g — ¼ cup) self-raising flour (or plain flour plus ½ level tsp baking powder), 2 oz (50 g — ¾ cup) finely shredded suet, salt and pepper. Stir in just enough cold water (roughly 3 tbsps) to make a firm dough. Divide into 8 portions with a fork and place on top of the mince. Cover and cook for 20 minutes.

FORFAR BRIDIES

Reputed to have been "invented" by a Forfar baker in the 1850's and to be found now in every Scottish baker's shop—those with one hole in the top are "plain" bridies and those with two holes include onion. (This may vary according to location.)

Sift 1 lb (450 g — 4 cups) plain flour and ½ level tsp (½ x 5 ml spoon—½ tsp) salt into a mixing bowl. Add enough water (roughly 8 fl oz (225 ml—1 cup)) to make a stiff dough. Divide dough into four and roll out each piece on a floured surface to make an oval shape, at least 8″ x 5″ (20 x 13 cms).

Divide ¾ lb (350 g — 12 oz) raw minced steak into four and place on one half of each oval of pastry. Remove skin from 2 oz (50 g — 2 oz) fresh suet, chop it finely and mix with 1 finely chopped onion. Sprinkle suet and onion over meat and season with salt and pepper. Fold pastry in two lengthwise, pinch edges together to seal well and flute edges. Place bridies flat on a greased baking sheet, make a small hole in the centre of each to allow steam to escape.

Bake in a hot oven (425°F/220°C — mark 7) for about ½ hour—the pastry should be biscuit coloured.

BEEF AND BEAN DUMPLING

One of the many variations on the "mince and tatties" theme and a real hungry-family favourite.

Ingredients	Imperial	Metric	American
Suet Pastry:			
Self-raising flour (or plain flour plus baking powder)	8 oz	225 gms	2 cups
baking powder	1 level tsp	1 x 5 ml spoon	1 tsp
Salt	¼ level tsp	¼ x 5 ml spoon	¼ tsp
Shredded suet	4 oz	125 gms	¾ cup
Cold water	3 fl oz	75 ml	6 tbsps
Filling:			
Minced steak	1 lb	450 gms	1 lb
Mixed with 1 finely chopped onion and 1 tin baked beans in tomato sauce	15 oz	425 gms	15 oz
Salt and pepper			

To make the suet pastry, sift dry ingredients into a mixing bowl, stir in suet and gradually add enough cold water to make a firm dough. Reserve a third of the dough for the top of the pudding. On a floured surface, roll out remaining ⅔rds into a large circle, about ¼″ (¾ cm) thick. Grease a 2 pint (litre — 5 cup) pudding basin and gently ease in the circle of pastry, pressing it to the sides of the basin. Mix filling ingredients together and put into the pastry lined basin. Roll out reserved pastry to fit the top of the basin and put it in place, pinching edges of pastry together to seal well. Cover with a snap-on lid or with foil, allowing room for the dumpling to rise.

Place basin in several inches of boiling water in a large saucepan. Cover pan and steam for 2 hours.

BOILED SILVERSIDE OF BEEF

Serves 4 people for 2 days plus soup

Ingredients	Imperial	Metric	American
Piece of silverside, trimmed of fat, water to cover	3 lbs	1¼ kg	3 lbs
Salt	2 tsps	2 x 5 ml spoons	2 tsps
6 peppercorns			
6 allspice berries (optional)			
1 onion, stuck with 4 cloves			
2 carrots			
Small piece turnip			
Small piece bay leaf			
Large sprig parsley, with stalks			
Extra carrots, to eat with the meat	1 lb	450 gms	1 lb

Bring slowly to the boil, cover and simmer for 3 hours. Add whole carrots during last 30 mins. Remove beef and eat hot with dumplings, carrots and boiled potatoes—or press under a weighted plate and eat cold next day.

DUMPLINGS

Ingredients	Imperial	Metric	American
Self-raising flour	4 oz	125 gms	1 cup flour plus ½ tsp baking powder
Shredded suet	2 oz	50 gms	⅜ cup
Salt and pepper			
Cold water to mix	about 2 fl oz	50 ml	4 tbsps

20 minutes before serving meat, remove some stock to a separate pan. Mix dumpling ingredients together and drop in tbsps into the boiling stock. Cover and simmer until dumplings are well risen—about 15 mins.

31

BOUILLON

The remaining stock makes excellent beef bouillon for serving next day. Strain liquor in which meat was cooked, cover and chill overnight. Skim off fat, strain into a saucepan. To clear soup, add the white and shell of one egg and bring to the boil. Simmer 1 hour and strain through a piece of fine cloth placed over a sieve. (Freezer owners will find it useful to store some of this strong stock for soups or in stews. Freeze in ice cube trays, then overwrap.)

POTTED BEEF

Makes about 1¼ lbs

Ingredients	Imperial	Metric	American
Stewing steak (lean as possible)	1¼ lbs	575 gms	1¼ lbs
Salt and pepper			
1 crushed clove garlic or 1 small onion, finely chopped			
Melted butter	½ oz	15 gms	1 tbsp

Cut steak into smallish pieces and remove all fat. Sprinkle with salt and pepper and put into a 2 pint casserole with garlic or onion. Just cover with water, cover and cook in a slow oven (250°F/130°C—mark 2) until very tender—about 2½ hours. Allow to cool, then pass through the fine blade of a mincing machine. Moisten with 5 tbsps (5 x 15 ml spoons—5 tbsps) of the meat juices in the casserole, then press into a dish of suitable size. Seal with the melted butter.

Serve with rolls or crusty bread and salad for high tea and snacks or "help yourself" outdoor eating. As a sandwich spread, use on its own or blended with a little mayonnaise.

POT ROAST OF BEEF WITH VEGETABLES

Serves 4-6

Ingredients	Imperial	Metric	American
Mixed fresh vegetables (e.g. carrot, turnip, onion), prepared weight	1½ lbs	675 gms	1½ lbs
Piece of beef without bone (e.g. silverside or brisket)	2 lbs	1 kg	2 lbs
Cooking oil OR	2 tbsps	2 x 15 ml spoons	2 tbsps
Fat	1 oz	25 gms	2 tbsps
Salt and pepper			
Hot water or stock	½ pint	275 ml	1¼ cups

Peel and dice vegetables. Brown meat quickly on all sides in the hot oil or fat, then sprinkle with salt and pepper. Set meat on top of vegetables in a deep casserole. Pour in hot water or stock, cover and cook in a very moderate oven (350°F/180°C—mark 3) until meat is tender—2 to 2½ hours. Transfer beef to a hot serving dish and thicken gravy, if desired, with browning—alternatively, vegetables and liquid can be pureed to make a naturally thickened sauce.

Serve with creamed potatoes. Some horseradish sauce makes a zesty accompaniment.

ROAST BEEF—FOR SERVING COLD

This is a very economical method which enables you to cook a small roast with an absolute minimum of shrinkage and produces juicy, tender meat just tinged with pink in the centre. If you like your beef very "well done", allow 20 mins. extra cooking time.

Wrap 1½ lbs (675 g—1½ lbs) rolled sirloin of beef in foil, set this on a rack in a roasting tin. Place in a pre-heated, very mod oven (325°F/170°C—mark 3) for 1½ hours. Allow to cool in the foil and slice when completely cold.

SCOTCH BEEF OLIVES WITH VEGETABLES

If your butcher will slice the meat for you on his bacon cutter, so much the better.

Ingredients	Imperial	Metric	American
Lean steak, sliced thin (preferably rump, topside or round steak)	1 lb	450 gms	1 lb
Oatmeal stuffing:			
Oatmeal or loose oats	4 oz	125 gms	1 cup
1 small onion chopped fine			
Salt	1 tsp	1 x 5 ml spoon	1 tsp
Pepper			
Butter or margarine	2 oz	50 gms	¼ cup
Dripping or cooking fat	2 oz	50 gms	¼ cup
1 large onion, chopped			
Flour	2 tbsps	2 x 15 ml spoons	2 tbsps
1 carrot, peeled and sliced			
1 small piece yellow turnip, cut into large dice			
1 Oxo or beef stock cube			
Hot water	1 pint	575 ml	2½ cups
Salt and pepper to taste			

Cut the beef into portions, roughly postcard size, and beat until thin and flat. Prepare the oatmeal stuffing by mixing the oatmeal, chopped onion, salt and pepper together in a bowl and rubbing in the butter. Place some of the stuffing on each piece of meat, roll up and tie each beef olive securely with linen thread or thin string.

Melt the dripping in a skillet or heavy-based saucepan and brown the beef olives and the chopped onion; sprinkle with the flour. Crumble the oxo cube into the hot water and add to the pan; stir and allow to bubble up, then reduce the heat. Add the prepared vegetables, cover and simmer gently until beef is tender—1½ to 2 hours. Season to taste.

Serve with creamy, mashed potatoes.

BRAWN

This recipe uses a pig's head—sheep's head and ox head were much used in days gone by but would be somewhat difficult to come by now.

Ingredients	Imperial	Metric	American
½ a pig's head			
2 pig's trotters			
1 lb shin beef	1 lb	450 gms	1 lb
1 nap (thin end of shin) bone			
Salt and pepper, to taste			
2 bay leaves, 6 cloves, blade of mace			
(optional) and sprig of thyme			

The pig's head will be cleaned (brains removed, etc.) when bought. Wash it very thoroughly and put it in a large pan with remaining ingredients. Cover with cold water and bring to the boil. Cover and cook until very tender—about 1½ hours. Remove all meat from the bones and strain liquid through a sieve. Put meat, finely chopped, and strained liquid back into the pot and simmer for 3 hours more. When cool, turn into a mould, bowl or tin and leave to set.

Slice when cold and serve with pickles or salad.

HAGGIS

Innocents abroad in Scotland should take no notice of the "Beware—Haggis Crossing" signs to be seen in the Western Highlands. No haggis has ever been known to cross an open road. Visitors should also treat with scorn any excuse that haggis is "out of season"—it never is.

I prefer to cook my haggis in a bowl, as do most modern Scots, rather than in a scalded and scraped sheep's stomach. You can, of course, buy genuine skin-clad haggis from any Scottish butcher or even in tins but with all due respect, I consider this home-made version, using only the most acceptable innards, even better.

Makes 2 large haggis, each serving 6. (Can be deep frozen up to 3 months.)

Ingredients	Imperial	Metric	American
Sheep's or ox heart, without fat or tubes	1 lb	450 gms	1 lb
Sheep's or ox liver	1 lb	450 gms	1 lb
Stewing steak, without fat	½ lb	225 gms	½ lb
Shredded or finely minced suet	4 oz	125 gms	¾ cup
Onion, grated	2 large	2 large	2 large
Salt	2 level tsps	2 x 5 ml spoons	2 tsps
Black pepper, good sprinkling freshly ground	¼ level tsp	¼ x 5 ml spoon	¼ tsp
Coarse oatmeal	½ lb	225 gms	2 cups

Blend all ingredients thoroughly. Lightly press into two well-greased, 1¾-2 pint bowls (1 litre or 1 American quart). Cover with snap-on lids or with foil or buttered paper tied round the rim with string. Steam in a large pan for 2½ to 3 hours. The simmering water should come half way up the bowls and be replenished as necessary to maintain this level.

Serve with "bashed neeps and tatties" (well mashed turnip and potatoes). A good, thick beef or lamb-stock gravy goes well with haggis too.

To serve on Burns Night (January 25)

The haggis should, of course, be piped in to the tune of "Scotland The Brave" or something of that ilk, held aloft on a silver tray. The piper himself should, if at all possible, be arrayed in full highland regalia. My husband is often called upon to perform this pleasant duty and tells me that the nip of whisky which is the piper's traditional reward is almost a necessity, after such effort. The chairman of the gathering then gives the toast to the Haggis* and makes the first cut in it.

After the meal has been eaten and a suitable amount of whisky consumed, a chosen guest gives an appropriate address—for example, tales of Rabbie Burns or a marathon recital of the Bard's "Tam-o-Shanter".

*"ADDRESS TO A HAGGIS" (Burns)

Fair fa' your honest, sonsie face
Great chieftain o' the puddin race!
Aboon them a' ye tak your place,
  Painch, tripe, or thairm.
Weel are ye wordy o' a grace
  As lang's my airm.

HIGHLAND SAUSAGE CASSEROLE

Ingredients	Imperial	Metric	American
Beef sausages	1 lb	450 gms	1 lb
Oatmeal or loose oats	2 oz	50 gms	½ cup
1 large onion, sliced			
Carrots, sliced	½ lb	225 gms	1 cup
Turnip, diced	¼ lb	125 gms	½ cup
Tomato purée, mixed with	2 tbsps	2 x 15 ml spoons	2 tbsps
boiling water	½ pint	275 ml	1¼ cups

Place sausages in a casserole—do not prick the skins. Just cover the base of the casserole with cold water, put on the lid and place in a moderate oven (375°F/190°C—mark 5) for half an hour.

Drain off liquid and fat. Sprinkle oats over the sausages and add remaining ingredients. Recover the casserole and return it to the oven until vegetables are tender—about 30 mins.

Serve with plain boiled or mashed potatoes.

BRAISED OXTAIL

Ingredients	Imperial	Metric	American
1 Ox tail, jointed			
Seasoned flour	1 oz	25 gms	3 tbsps
Cooking fat	2 oz	50 gms	¼ cup
1 large onion, peeled and sliced			
2 medium sized carrots, diced small			
1 stick celery or small piece of turnip, finely chopped			
1 tin condensed beef consommé jellied			
Additional thickening—butter	1 oz	25 gms	2 tbsps
flour	1 level tbsp	1 x 15 ml spoon	1 tbsps

Have your butcher joint the oxtail into sections. Coat the pieces of oxtail in the seasoned flour. Melt the fat in a thick stewpan and brown the oxtail in it. Remove the meat from the pan while you gently fry the prepared vegetables for 3 minutes. Return the oxtail to the pan with the vegetables, add the undiluted beef consommé. Reduce heat to the lowest possible simmering point, cover the pan and let it simmer very gently for 2-3 hours, checking occasionally to make sure all the liquid has not been absorbed and adding a little water, if necessary. At the end of cooking time, the oxtail meat should be so tender that it flakes easily from the bone. If you wish to thicken the gravy put butter and flour on a flat plate and work together with a fork to form a thick paste. Add this, one small piece at a time, to the pan until the gravy thickens, stirring it very gently so as not to break up the meat.

PORK AND KALE (Modern Version)

The old way was to cook a whole roll of pickled pork or bacon in more water and to use the resulting "bree" or liquid as soup. This is a one-pot dish which probably used to be cooked over an open fire, so that it was a good way of producing meat, potatoes and a green vegetable at the same time for supper. "Kale", in Orkney, is what we mainlanders call cabbage.

In a large saucepan, fry as many bacon rashers as needed per person, using a little lard, dripping or butter. Add small, whole potatoes or larger potatoes cut to equal size and roughly chopped cabbage, to feed the same number of people. Pour in water to come ½" (1½ cm) up the pan and sprinkle with salt and (optional) dill seeds. Bring to the boil, cover and cook gently until potatoes are tender, by which time all or most of the liquid will be absorbed.

PRESSED OX TONGUE

Serves 8

Ingredients	Imperial	Metric	American
1 ox tongue, weighing about	2½ lbs	1¼ kg	2½ lbs
1 onion			
1 stalk celery			
1 carrot			
8 peppercorns			
1 bay leaf			
Salt — 2 level tsps *only* if tongue is bought unsalted			
Water to cover			
Gelatin	1 level tsp	1 x 5 ml spoon	1 tsp

Wash tongue and soak overnight in cold water. Put tongue into a large saucepan and cover with fresh cold water, plus remaining stock ingredients. Bring to boil and simmer until tender — 30 minutes to the lb (½ kg) plus 30 minutes extra. Cool. Skin and remove small bones, gristle and fat. Press into a straight sided dish or cake tin just big enough to take the tongue when curled round.

Sprinkle gelatin over ¼ pint (150 ml — 10 tbsps) of strained stock and dissolve. Use just enough to level with the top of the tongue. Set a smaller tin or dish on top and weight it down. Leave in a refrigerator or cool place overnight. Turn out and slice thin when cold.

POTTED HOUGH

All Scottish butchers worth their salt sell their own make of potted hough — almost invariably in half-pint, fluted moulds. It is very easy to make at home too.

Ingredients	Imperial	Metric	American
Hough (shin beef), on the bone —the "nap" end is preferable	**2-2½ lbs**	**1 kg**	**2-2½ lbs**
Blade of mace and 3-4 whole cloves (both optional)			
Salt and pepper			
Water			

Ask the butcher to break the bone through for you. Wash and place the meat, still on the bone, in a large pan and just cover with cold water. Add spices, if used, and bring slowly to the boil. Simmer very gently, skimming occasionally, for at least six hours — the meat should literally fall from the bones. (In the old days, it would be left to simmer all night on the solid fuel range.) Strain the stock into a bowl. Remove all fat and gristle from the bones and either mince or finely chop the meat into another bowl. Cover both bowls and leave in a cool place overnight.

Next day, skim solidified fat from the top of the stock and put it into a pan with the meat. Bring to the boil and simmer ten minutes. Season well. Cool and pour into wetted moulds, then leave to set.

Unmould before serving and serve with salad or pickles.

STROMNESS STEAK

Allow one steak per person — sirloin, topside, T bone or fillet is best, cutting it ½" to ¾" (1½ to 2 cm) thick. Season with freshly ground pepper (no salt at this stage) and brush with melted butter on one side, then dip this side in flaked or porridge oats. Turn steak and repeat seasoning and dipping process on the other side.

Fry in butter for 3 minutes on each side — 5 minutes each side if you like it very "well done" — turning only once. Sprinkle with plain or garlic salt. Turn heat low.

Flame steaks in malt whisky, thus — put 1 tbsp (1 x 15 ml spoon — 1 tbsp) whisky per person into a small pan, heat and set the whisky alight. Pour flaming whisky over steaks in the pan and shake pan gently over heat until flames die down. Be ready to serve steaks immediately, with clapshot (Page 61)

38

LAMB

Scotch quality lamb is now branded as such, to guarantee both origin and consistent top quality—it certainly ranks amongst the finest lamb produced anywhere in the world. Leg of lamb is called "gigot" of lamb in Scotland (shades of the "Auld Alliance" with France) and the prime cuts, properly cooked and presented, are fit for a banquet while the cheaper cuts make economical but no less tasty stews, pies and casseroles. The natural sweetness of lamb blends with many flavourings and accompaniments—try adding a hint of rosemary, garlic, thyme or dried dill in the cooking, freshly chopped chives and parsley as a garnish, caper sauce or redcurrant jelly as an alternative to mint sauce.

Roasting Times: These are approximate, since much depends on the size, shape and quality of the meat, and should produce meat which is moist, juicy and slightly pink in the centre, with a minimum of shrinkage:—

Prime cuts (leg, shoulder, loin, saddle) — Medium to Well Done—30 to 35 Allow 8-12 oz (225-350 g—8-12 oz) mins per lb at 350°F/180°C with bone, per person. mark 4

Boned, rolled or stuffed joints, Allow — Well Done—45 to 50 mins per lb 4-6 oz (125-175 g—4-6 oz) per person, at 350°F/180°C—mark 4 without bone

BREADED LAMB CHOPS

Ingredients	Imperial	Metric	American
4 loin of lamb chops about thick 1″		**2½ cm**	**1″**
Flour seasoned with salt and pepper			
1 egg, beaten			
Dry breadcrumbs to coat			
Butter ⎫ to fry	1 oz	25 gms	2 tbsps
Oil ⎬	2 tbsps	2 x 15 ml spoons	2 tbsps

Trim any excess fat from the chops. Dip first in seasoned flour, then in beaten egg and finally in fine, dry crumbs, to coat thoroughly.

Heat butter and oil until sizzling in a thick frying pan. Put in the chops and fry for 6 to 9 mins on each side, depending on whether or not you like them to be tinged with pink in the middle. Use only medium heat throughout cooking, so that crumb coating remains brown but not burnt before the centre of the chops has cooked.

Serve with new potatoes and green peas. To taste new potatoes at their very best, cook in their skins, then slip the skins off and toss potatoes in a little butter and finely chopped mint.

STUFFED LAMB CUTLETS

This is made from best end of neck, boned, stuffed and roasted in one piece then cut into cutlets.

Serves 6

Ingredients	Imperial	Metric	American
Best end neck of lamb—ask the butcher to bone it for you	3 lbs	1¼ kgs	3 lbs
Stuffing:			
Pork sausage meat	¼ lb	125 gms	¼ lb
Chopped parsley and mint	1 level tsp	1 x 5 ml spoon	1 tsp
Shredded suet (e.g. Atora)	2 oz	50 gms	⅜ cup
4 'blades' finely chopped rosemary			
OR dried rosemary	¼ tsp	¼ x 5 ml spoon	¼ tsp
Strained apple sauce	1 tbsp	1 x 15 ml spoon	1 tbsp
Chestnut or tomato purée	1 tbsp	1 x 15 ml spoon	1 tbsp
Fresh white breadcrumbs	3 oz	75 gms	1½ cups
Salt and pepper			
1 egg			

Lay boned lamb flat and sprinkle lightly with salt and pepper. Blend stuffing ingredients and spread over the meat. Roll up and tie lightly at 1″ (2½ cms) intervals with string. Place on a rack in a roasting tin and cook in a moderate oven (375°F/190°C — mark 5) for 40 minutes per lb (450 g or ½ kg — lb) basting occasionally.

Before serving, cut into cutlets between each "tie" and remove string. Serve with gravy and mint sauce. Good vegetables to go with the cutlets are roast or new potatoes, green peas and lightly fried mushrooms.

SPRING-COATED LAMB

A succulent roast of lamb with the added interest of a crisp, crumb-and-herb coating makes fine Easter fare. Bring the joint to the table on a bed of fresh, green rosemary, if you have it in the garden, and tuck a small sprig of it under the meat while it is roasting.

Serves 8 (Allow ½ lb (225 g — ½ lb) per person, when ordering).
Cooking time—35-40 minutes per lb (225 g — lb)

Ingredients	Imperial	Metric	American
Leg of lamb	4 lbs	1¾ kgs	4 lbs

Ingredients	Imperial	Metric	American
Coating:			
Fine, fresh breadcrumbs	**6 oz**	**175 gms**	**3 cups**
1 clove garlic or garlic salt (optional)			
Salt and pepper			
Fresh thyme leaves OR ¼ level tsp dried thyme	**½ level tsp**	**½ x 5 ml spoon**	**½ tsp**
Finely chopped parsley	**2 tbsps**	**2 x 15 ml spoons**	**2 tbsp**
Finely grated lemon rind from ½ lemon			

Pre-heat oven to 350°F/180°C — mark 4 and place meat in the centre of it, set on a rack in a roasting tin. Prepare crumbs and spread them out thinly on a baking sheet, then place in the oven to become thoroughly dry—10 minutes or so should be enough. Place garlic in roasting tin, beneath meat.

20 minutes before the end of roasting time, increase heat to 400°F/200°C — mark 6) and remove roast from oven. Cut away outer skin, taking care not to remove the underlying fat. Combine breadcrumbs with seasoning, including garlic salt, thyme, parsley and rind and spread this mixture over the roast. Return roast to the oven until coating is golden brown.

Serve with gravy made from pan drippings. I would choose red currant jelly rather than mint sauce as an accompaniment in this case, plus creamed or roast potatoes, carrots and a green vegetable.

LAMB IN ASPIC

Cut 1 lb (450 g—1 lb) cooked, lean lamb into small dice. Make up 1 pint (575 ml—2½ cups) aspic jelly according to directions on packet. Pour enough into a wetted, 6″ (15 cm) cake tin to form a thin layer on the base and allow this to set. Arrange some of the meat and slices of tomato in a design on the bottom of the tin, first dipping each piece into a little of the aspic jelly. When this has set, gently spoon in another thin layer of aspic.

Mix remaining meat and aspic, plus half a cup of lightly cooked green peas and 1 level tbsp of finely chopped mint together in a bowl. Set the bowl on ice, stirring occasionally until it begins to set, then turn mixture into the tin. Leave several hours or overnight to become quite firm. Unmould and garnish with watercress and/or cucumber slices.

SAVOURY SHEPHERD'S PIE (Using cooked lamb)

Ingredients	Imperial	Metric	American
1 small onion, chopped			
Mushrooms, washed and chopped	**2 oz**	**50 gms**	**2 oz**
Dripping or cooking fat	**½ oz**	**15 gms**	**1 tbsps**
Minced or finely chopped cooked lamb	**1 lb**	**450 gms**	**1 lb**

Ingredients	Imperial	Metric	American
Dash Worcestershire sauce			
Gravy	about ½ pint	275 ml	1¼ cups
Salt and pepper			
Mashed potatoes	1 lb	225 gms	1 lb

Fry the onion and mushrooms gently in the dripping or fat, for 2-3 mins. Add meat, sauce, gravy and seasoning. When thoroughly heated through, turn into an oven dish and pile or pipe mashed potatoes on top. Brush with a little beaten egg (optional) and bake in a moderately hot oven (400°F/200°C— mark 6) until nicely ridged with brown.

CROWN ROAST OF LAMB

An excellent roast which looks extremely attractive for a large dinner party.

Serves 6-8

Ask your butcher to prepare the crown for you from two best-end necks of lamb (8-12 cutlets). The backbone is chopped through and a slice made between each cutlet to about half-way down. The bones can then be bent backwards and outwards and the meat is skewered or tied together in the shape of a crown. The ends of the cutlet bones are scraped free of meat and trimmed to a sharp point.

Sprinkle the inside of the roast with salt and pepper, rub with a cut clove garlic (optional) and place on a rack in a roasting tin. Wrap the tips of the bones with small pieces of foil to prevent burning. Roast in a very moderate oven (350°F/180°C—mark 4) until tender.

When cooked, fill centre of the roast with prepared stuffing (e.g. Bread and Herb Stuffing or Herb Rice) or with cooked spring vegetables, topped by piped mashed potatoes and garnished with green peas.

Before serving, fit a paper cutlet frill onto the end of each bone or alternate frills with stuffed green olives.

POT ROASTED LAMB, with Mint Sauce

This rolled shoulder roast is lightly flavoured with either rosemary or dill and has a bland, mushroom stuffing. Allow ½ lb (225 g—½ lb) shoulder lamb per person, boned weight.

Ingredients	Imperial	Metric	American
Boned shoulder of lamb			
Mushrooms	4 oz	125 gms	4 oz
Butter	1 oz	25 gms	2 tbsps
Finely chopped parsley	2 tbsps	2 x 15 ml spoons	2 tbsps

42

Ingredients	Imperial	Metric	American
Salt and pepper			
Good pinch dried rosemary or dill seeds (or 3 or 4 short stalks fresh rosemary)			
Flour seasoned with salt and pepper or cayene			
Cooking fat or oil	1 oz	25 gms	2 tbsps
2 stalks celery, with leaves			
Water or light stock	½ pint	275 ml	1¼ cups
1 small close garlic, crushed with salt (optional)			

Ask your butcher to prepare the lamb for rolling but to leave it untied. Finely chop mushrooms and fry them gently for 2 mins. in butter. Spread mushrooms over inside surface of lamb and sprinkle with parsley, salt and pepper. Roll up tightly and tie with string at 1″ intervals. Rub outer surface with dried rosemary or dill seeds, or put the fresh rosemary stalks on top and on either side of the lamb at a later stage. Dredge the roast with seasoned flour.

Heat fat or oil in a large pan or flameproof casserole. Brown the meat in it briskly. Add celery, cut into 1″ (2½ cm) pieces, and the stock or water. Bring to the boil. Transfer to a casserole, if necessary. Add fresh rosemary and garlic, if used. Cover and cook in a very moderate oven (350°F/180°C—mark 4) until tender—allow 45 mins to each lb (½ kg), stuffed weight. The gravy should be strained, then thickened if you wish, and served separately.

Accompany with buttery mashed potatoes, a green vegetable and either freshly made or bought mint sauce.

FRESH MINT SAUCE

Pluck a good handful of mint leaves from the stem and wash. Put onto a chopping board and sprinkle with caster sugar—about 1 tsp (1 x 5 ml spoon—1 tsp). Chop finely—the sugar will be absorbed by the juice from the mint. Let stand for 10 mins then place in a small dish and add vinegar to taste.

ONE-DISH LAMB STEW

Ingredients	Imperial	Metric	American
Shoulder lamb, without bone	1½ lbs	675 gms	1½ lbs
2 Onions			
2 Carrots			
2 Parsnips			
Peeled potatoes	1 lb	450 gms	1 lb
Flour seasoned with salt and pepper and (optional) garlic powder	1½ oz	5 x 15 ml spoons	5 tbsps
3 tbsps cooking oil OR			
Fat	1½ oz	40 gms	3 tbsps
Water to cover			

Trim excess fat from lamb and cut into 1"-1½" (2½-4 cm) pieces. Chop onions, slice carrots and parsnips, dice turnip. Halve or quarter potatoes to make them even-sized.

Turn lamb in seasoned flour, to coat, then brown in hot oil or fat in a fairly large saucepan or stove-top casserole. Add prepared vegetables and pour in enough hot water to cover. Cover pan and cook until lamb is tender, either on top of the stove or in a very moderate oven (325°F/170°C—mark 2 to 3).

SHEPHERD'S PIE

Ingredients	Imperial	Metric	American
Cooking fat	**1 oz**	**25 gms**	**2 tbsps**
Raw minced beef	**1 lb**	**450 gms**	**1 lb**
1 Large onion chopped			
2 carrots diced small			
Salt and pepper to taste			
Potatoes	**1 lb**	**450 gms**	**1 lb**
Knob of butter			

Melt the fat in a heavy saucepan and brown the minced beef and chopped onion in it, over a medium heat; lower heat, add diced carrot, salt and pepper; cover and simmer for 15 minutes. Meanwhile, peel, quarter and boil the potatoes in salted water, then drain and mash them with a little butter. Turn the meat into a buttered pie dish or casserole and spread the mashed potatoes over the top; decorate by scoring the mashed potatoes with a fork and place the pie in a pre-heated, hot oven (425°F/220°C — mark 7) for 10 minutes or so, until lightly browned. Serve piping hot.

SMALL MUTTON PIES

To be authentic, these should be made with "hot water pastry" but a quick, modern version can be made with ordinary short pastry, even the frozen kind.

Serves 6

Roll 12 oz (350 g — 12 oz) pastry out thinly on a floured surface. Using a 3¾" (9½ cms) cutter, cut 6 circles of pastry and use to line six greased, deep bun tins. Roll out trimmings and cut 6-3" (7½ cms) diameter circles, for the lids.

For the filling, cut up 8 oz (225 g — 8 oz) lean mutton into very small pieces and mix with 1 finely chopped onion. Add salt and pepper, a pinch of dried thyme (optional) and nutmeg and moisten with a little stock or water. Divide between tins. Brush pastry lids with cold water and set in position, then press edges of pastry firmly together to seal. Make a hole in the centre of the pies, brush with milk and bake in the centre of a moderately hot oven (400°F/200°C — mark 6) for 30 minutes. Serve very hot.

* *To make hot water pastry*, melt 2 oz beef dripping in 5 fl oz (150 ml — 10 tbsps) boiling water and pour into 8 oz (225 g — 2 cups) flour sifted with ½ level tsp (½ x 5 ml spoon — ½ tsp) salt. Mix with a fork, then knead smooth when cool enough to handle.

Game and Poultry

" . . . let us not fast owre lang,
But blithely spend what's blithely got."

(Very loosely ascribed to Rob Roy)

GAME, in Scotland, is in season roughly from mid-August until mid-March although pheasant and partridge are later — from the beginning of September to the beginning of February for the latter and from mid-October to 1st February for the former. In these days, of course, the deep freeze enables us to enjoy game all year round. Nevertheless, nothing is ever quite so good as when in its own natural season and the following table may be useful also as a guide to the best time to "stock up" for the deep freeze.

Ducklings — March to July
Ducks — always available but considered best July to February
Geese — October to March
Grouse — 12th August to end of February
Hare — 1st August to end of February
Partridges — 1st September to end of January
Pheasants — 15th October to end of January
Pigeons — always available
Rabbits — always available (now imported from China!)
Venison
    Buck — June to end of September
    Doe — November to end of January

BOILED FOWL WITH DILL OR CAPER SAUCE

Cook the fowl as in "Cock-a-Leekie Soup" recipe (page 10). Reserve half a pint (275 ml — 1¼ cups) of stock for this dish, using the rest in soup.

Having cooked the fowl, remove skin and bone and separate chicken meat into quite large, serving pieces. Place in a pan or casserole with the ½ pint (275 ml — 1¼ cups) of reserved stock and reheat while you make the sauce.

Melt 1½ oz (40 g — 3 tbsps) butter in a saucepan over gentle heat. Stir in 3 level tbsps (3 x 15 ml spoons) flour and stir for 2 minutes, taking care not to let the paste brown. Gradually add the hot stock (strained from the chicken, which should be kept warm) and enough creamy milk to make a thick, smooth sauce. Before serving, add 2 tbsps (2 x 15 ml spoons — 2 tbsps) chopped fresh dill leaves or drained, pickled capers, plus salt and pepper, to taste. Pour sauce over the chicken and serve with boiled rice.

PHEASANT WITH APPLES AND CREAM

Pre-cook the pheasant as in "Pheasant Pie" recipe on page 55. When cool, joint the bird, discard skin and bones and leave flesh in fairly large pieces, as before. Cover and set aside.

Finely chop one onion and fry this gently, along with one clove crushed garlic, in 2 oz (50 g — ¼ cup) butter. Peel, core and slice 3 medium sized cooking apples ¼″ (¾ cm) thick and add this to the pan. Turn and cook gently until softened and yellowed. Either purée the contents of the pan in an electric liquidiser or crush to a pulp with a potato masher. Season with salt, freshly ground pepper, then stir in 4 tbsps (4 x 15 ml — 4 tbsps) thick cream and 1 tbsp (1 x 15 ml — 1 tbsp) brandy or calvados. Check seasoning again and pour sauce over pheasant in a deep, warm dish. Garnish with sprigs of fresh rosemary, if available, and sections of unpeeled, green apple which have been dipped in lemon juice.

Serve with whole mushrooms, sautéed in butter and sprinkled with salt, freshly ground pepper and a little lemon juice.

ROAST PHEASANT

Hens are smaller but usually more tender than cocks. Hang the bird for 5-7 days, clean thoroughly, rinse in cold water and pat dry. Smear with butter and set on a rack in a roasting tin. (The bird can be stuffed, if you wish, with oatmeal or bread stuffing, with apples, cranberries, or simply a knob of butter.) Cook in a very moderate oven for 1-1½ hours or until tender; about ¼ pint (150 ml — 10 tbsps) red wine poured over the bird half way through cooking improves and moistens it. Serve with fried, buttered breadcrumbs and thinly sliced, deep-fried potatoes, and unthickened gravy from the pan drippings.

From August onwards, "Jugged Hare" is a specialty you may be offered in Scotland and is a feast to hold its own with any of the classic dishes of the world. There is no short cut to preparing this splendid dish but it will be worth every moment you spend on it.

JUGGED HARE

Serves 6-8

(Allow 36 hours to marinade before cooking.)

Dressing Hare

Hares should be hung for up to 10 days (3 days is enough for my taste) and drawn just before use. When skinning the animal, do not puncture the membrane in the ribs which contains the blood. After skinning, drain off and keep blood for thickening the gravy.

Using 1 young hare, cut off the legs and chop each in two. Cut back in several pieces. (Rib cage can be simmered with neck in water for stock.) Put hare to soak in marinade for up to 36 hours, turning occasionally.

Marinade

Bring to the boil, then let cool — ¼ pint (150 ml — 10 tbsps) port or red wine, 2 tbsp (2 x 15 ml spoons — 2 tbsps) oil, 2 shallots or 1 small onion (chopped), juice of ½ lemon, 1 tsp (1 x 5 ml spoon — 1 tsp) chopped parsley, 1 bay leaf, salt and pepper, 6 crushed juniper berries. Remove hare from marinade and pat dry with kitchen paper.

47

Method of cooking

Fry 2 rashers chopped bacon in 2 tbsp (2 x 15 ml spoons — 2 tbsps) oil. Take out bacon and reserve. Brown the hare in the same pan then remove to a deep casserole. Add to the casserole 2 onions, each stuck with 2 cloves, and 2 carrots cut in quarters. Tie in a piece of muslin and add to the casserole — 10 whole allspice, 1 large sprig parsley, 1 small bayleaf and 1 sprig thyme. Return bacon to casserole. Just cover meat with strained marinade, plus stock or water 1½-2 pints (about 1 litre — 4½-5 cups). Add 8 peppercorns and salt to taste, the juice of ½ lemon and 2 small strips peel. Cover and cook in a slow oven (275°F/140°C — mark 1) until meat is thoroughly tender — 2½ to 3 hours.

Drain off all the gravy into a saucepan. Discard vegetables and muslin bag contents.

Thicken gravy as follows —

Make a "beurre manié" by combining 1½ oz (40 g — 3 tbsps) butter and 1¼ oz (4 x 15 ml spoons — 4 tbsps) flour into a paste — use the flat of a knife on a plate. Add a piece of this paste at a time to the gravy and bring to the boil. Remove from heat. Add enough blood from the hare to thicken nicely. Stir in ¼ pint (150 ml — 10 tbsps) port or red wine and 1 tbsp (1 x 15 ml spoon — 1 tbsp) redcurrant jelly. Return to heat until jelly dissolves.

ROAST VENISON

A 6 lb (approx. 3 kg — 6 lb) haunch of venison (with bone) serves 12 generously. Allow 6-8 oz (175-225 g — 6-8 oz) per person and 20 to 25 minutes per lb (½ kg — lb) roasting time to produce a "medium rare" roast.

For the marinade:

About ¼ pint (150 ml — 10 tbsps) red wine (Elderberry is excellent or any rich red wine)
3-4 tbsps olive or corn oil
3-4 strips thinly pared lemon peel
Sprinkling of salt and freshly ground black pepper
2 shallots or 1 small onion, chopped
Herbs—e.g. large sprig parsley, with stalks, sprig thyme, 6 crushed juniper berries, few blades rosemary

Soak the venison in the marinade for 24-48 hours, turning once, in a covered dish in a cool place or refrigerator. (Reserve marinade).

Place meat on a rack in a roasting tin and cook in a moderately hot oven (400°F/200°C — mark 6) for 20 minutes per lb (½ kg — lb) plus 20 minutes extra, turning once and drizzling melted butter on each side. This will produce a roast slightly pink in the middle, which is how venison tastes best.

To make the gravy, pour off all but 1 tbsp (1 x 15 ml spoon — 1 tbsp) of fat from the roasting tin. Add to the fat left in the tin the strained marinade (first brought to the boil) and 1 tbsp (1 x 15 ml spoon — 1 tbsp) redcurrant or other tart jelly. Bring to the boil and simmer until reduced. Serve with forcemeat balls, redcurrant jelly (or a mixture of redcurrant jelly and cranberry sauce is very good) and creamed potatoes, braised celery and buttered carrots.

Forcemeat Balls:

To about 4 oz (125 g — 2 cups) of soft breadcrumbs, add approx. 2 tbsps (2 x 15 ml spoons — 2 tbsps) each of finely chopped onion, celery, green pepper, apple and parsley; add a pinch of thyme, salt and pepper and bind with beaten egg. Form into ¾" (2 cm) balls and roll in flour. Deep or shallow fry in oil.

N.B. Be sure to reserve some leftovers for venison pasties. Cold venison, thinly sliced, is also excellent with salads.

VENISON PASTIES

It is a great boon to have some left-over, cooked venison with which to make these pasties—they are a real delicacy, and excellent either hot or cold.

Roll out 12 oz (350 g — 12 oz) short pastry (if home-made, use 6 oz (175 g — 1½ cups) flour, 3 oz (75 g — ⅜ cup) lard, a pinch of salt and cold water to bind) on a floured surface. Cut four circles, using a small teaplate as a guide.
    Mix about 8 oz (225 g — 8 oz) chopped, cooked venison with one medium-sized, grated raw onion and one smallish, grated raw carrot, plus enough gravy or stock to moisten. Season with salt and pepper. Divide filling between pastry rounds. Moisten edges with cold water, fold over into two and pinch and flute edges together. Place, with fluted edges uppermost, on a greased baking sheet. Brush with milk and bake in a moderately hot oven (400°F/ 200°C — mark 6) until nicely browned—about 20 to 25 minutes.

VENISON CASSEROLES OR PUFF PASTRY PIES

The cheaper (stewing) cuts of venison make very flavourful dishes, given patient, slow cooking. Cook the meat as in "Hunter's Hot Pot" recipe, page 51 adding a little more liquid, as required. When making a deep pie, first pre-cook the meat like this, then allow to cool before topping with a puff pastry lid. Brush this with beaten egg, add pastry leaves and cut a hole in the centre for steam to escape. Bake in a hot oven (425°F/220°C — mark 7) until well browned—about 20 minutes.

VENISON STEAKS

Venison steaks, cut about ½″ (1¼ cm) thick from the loin or haunch, can be fried or grilled, just as beef steaks. First, brush with a little oil or melted butter and place on a rack in the grill pan, about 1½ to 2″ (4-5 cm) away from the heat. They will take 3 to 5 minutes to grill on each side (and the same to fry) for medium rare to "well done" steaks. Garnish with watercress, when in season, or parsley and serve with mushrooms and a green vegetable. Season steaks with a little salt and pepper after cooking.

PARTRIDGE

A partridge will not usually weigh much more than 1 lb (450 g — 1 lb) and is therefore sufficient for only one to two portions. Cover the breast with fat bacon and roast in a moderately hot oven (400°F/200°C — mark 6) for 25 to 30 minutes, basting occasionally. Garnish with cress or parsley. Serve with fried potatoes and/or breadcrumbs and green salad.

GAME PIE

Any game bird—partridge, pheasant, pigeon, guinea fowl—can be used, by themselves or in combination with each other. The total weight of the dressed birds should be 3 to 3½ lbs (1¼-1½ kg — 3-3½ lbs).

Serves 6

Ingredients	Imperial	Metric	American
For the pastry:			
Plain flour	12 oz	350 gms	1½ cups
Salt	¼ level tsp	¼ x 5 ml spoon	¼ tsp
Hot water	¼ pint	150 ml	10 tbsps
Lard	4 oz	125 gms	½ cup
1 beaten egg			
For the filling:			
Game bird or birds	3½ lbs	1¼-1½ kgs	3-3½ lbs
Lean boned pork)	½ lb	225 gms	½ lb
Lean boned veal) or 1lb pork-½kg	½ lb	225 gms	½ lb
Pinch of ground allspice or sage			
Salt and pepper			
Stock made from the game bones	¼ pint	150 ml	10 tbsps

In the absence of a special pie mould, use a round cake tin 6″ to 7″ (15-18cm) in diameter. Grease the tin well.

Sift flour and salt together into a large bowl. Bring the water and lard to the boil in a small saucepan. Make a well in the flour, pour in the hot water and melted lard and mix together. Turn onto a floured surface and knead until smooth. Using two-thirds of the dough, roll out to ¼" (¾ cm) thick and carefully line the tin with this. Roll out remaining dough into a circle which will fit the top of the tin—cover and set aside.

Cut the flesh from the jointed bird(s) into fairly small pieces. Put the bones in a saucepan, cover with cold water and add a little salt. Bring to the boil and simmer long enough to produce a good stock. Mince the pork and veal together and season with allspice or sage, salt and pepper. Line the base and sides of the pie with the minced meat, then fill the centre with the game flesh, seasoning each layer. Moisten with a little of the stock. (The filling should come to the top of the pastry). Moisten edges of pastry with cold water, put on pastry lid and pinch edges together, to seal. Trim, flute edges and make a small hole in the centre of the lid, for steam to escape. Shape pastry trimmings into leaves to decorate the top. Brush pie with beaten egg, put leaves into position and brush those with egg.

Bake in a pre-heated, very moderate oven (350°F/180°C — mark 4) until centre filling is tender—2 to 2½ hours. Take from the oven and pour the (heated) remaining stock into the centre hole of the pie. Set aside in a cold place for two hours or longer. Serve completely cold.

HUNTER'S HOT POT
Serves 4-6

Ingredients	Imperial	Metric	American
1 good sized rabbit cut into serving pieces			
Flour, seasoned with salt (plain or garlic) and pepper	2 oz	50 gms	¼ cup
Cooking oil	4 tbsps	4 x 15 ml spoons	4 tbsps
2 rashers streaky bacon, diced			
Finely chopped parsley	1 tbsp	1 x 15 ml spoon	1 tbsp
6 crushed juniper berries (optional)			
Hot water or chicken stock	¼ pint	150 ml	10 tbsps
Tomato Purée	2 tbsps	2 x 15 ml spoons	2 tbsps
Potatoes	1½-2 lbs	¾-1 kg	1½-2 lbs
Butter, melted	1 oz	25 gms	1 tbsp

Toss the jointed rabbit in well seasoned flour, to coat thoroughly. Heat oil in a large pan or flameproof casserole and brown the rabbit pieces briefly. Transfer rabbit, if necessary, to a casserole and keep warm. Add diced bacon to pan in which rabbit was cooked and cook gently for 3 minutes. Stir in any remaining seasoned flour, parsley and juniper berries, if used, together with the blended hot water or stock and tomato purée. Bring to the boil and combine with rabbit. Cover casserole and cook in a very moderate oven (325°F/170°C — mark 3) for about 2½ hours or until rabbit is very tender.

Peel potatoes, put into cold, salted water and bring to the boil. Cook gently for 10 minutes only. Drain and when cool enough slice ¼″ (¾ cm) thick. Arrange in overlapping slices, on top of rabbit, during last 30 minutes cooking time, having drizzled melted butter over top. Increase heat to 450°F/230°C — mark 8) during last 10 minutes to brown potatoes.

Note: ¼ pint (150 ml — 10 tbsps) inexpensive red wine, added as part of the liquid content, makes a gourmet meal of this dish. Also, a teacupful of diced celery and carrots can be added to the meat in the casserole unless you prefer to serve a separate vegetable.

ROAST GROUSE

A plump, young grouse can be stuffed simply with a peeled onion and a small piece of butter, covered with bacon and roasted as for partridge. It should serve two adequately. Older birds are best casseroled and will take perhaps 1½ hours to become completely tender.

RABBIT CURRY

Rabbit meat, in a curry, is second to none. Joint the cleaned rabbit and turn the pieces in flour, seasoned with salt and pepper. Brown gently in 4 tbsps (4 x 15 ml spoons — 4 tbsps) cooking oil, then remove meat to the warmer.

Add a little more oil, if necessary, to the same pan and put in 1 large, chopped onion, 1 chopped, tart cooking apple (peeled and cored), and cook very gently until you can squash them down to a pulp with a potato masher. Stir in 1-3 level tbsps (1-3 x 15 ml spoons — 3 tbsps) curry powder, depending on how "hot" you like a curry to be. Cook over low heat for 3 minutes. Add the juice of half a lemon, 1 level tsp (1 x 5 ml — 1 tsp) salt, 1 oz (25 g — ¼ cup) dessicated coconut and 1 oz (25 g — ¼ cup) sultanas or raisins. Stir in ¾ pint (425 ml — 2 cups less 2 tbsps) hot water or chicken stock. Return rabbit to the pan. Reduce heat, cover the pan and simmer gently or cook in a slow oven (300°F/150°C — mark 2) until rabbit is fork tender.

Serve with plain boiled rice.

N.B. Tomato juice is very good either in place of the stock or as part of the liquid content.

PIGEON CASSEROLE

Brown two pigeons in about 1 oz (25 g — 2 tbsps) of bacon fat or butter. Remove pigeons from the pan and split them in two lengthwise, trimming away small pieces of bone and the backbone ridge with scissors. Place pigeon halves in a casserole in single layers.

In the same pan, gently fry 2 chopped rashers of bacon, then add them to the casserole. Add another oz of butter to the pan, let it melt and stir in 1 oz (25 g — 3 tbsps) flour. Let this brown, then gradually add ¾ pint (425 ml — 2 cups less 2 tbsps) chicken or ham stock and bring to the boil. Pour over pigeons in the casserole. Add 6 crushed juniper berries, a small bay leaf, 1 small clove crushed garlic, 2 strips thinly pared orange peel. Cover and cook in a slow oven (300°F/150°C — mark 2) for 1½ hours. Add 12 baby onions and 2 sliced carrots and cook 30 minutes longer. Thicken gravy, if preferred, and sprinkle with chopped parsley before serving with boiled rice or mashed potatoes.

RABBIT STEW

Ingredients	Imperial	Metric	American
Fat (bacon fat for preference)	1 oz	25 gms	2 tbsps
1 medium sized rabbit, jointed			
Flour, seasoned with salt and pepper	2 oz	50 gms	½ cup
Tomato juice	about 7 fl oz	200 ml	1 cup
Hot water	about ¾ pint	425 ml	2 cups
Pinch of dried tarragon (optional)			
Salt	½ level tsp	½ x 5 ml spoon	½ tsp

2 onions peeled and chopped
3 carrots peeled and sliced
1 small white turnip (or small piece yellow turnip) diced
1 small cauliflower, in sprigs

Melt the fat in a heavy stewpan. Coat the rabbit pieces with seasoned flour and brown it in the hot fat. Add tomato juice, water, tarragon, salt and onions and bring to the boil. Reduce the heat, cover the pan and simmer very gently for 50-60 minutes or until the rabbit is tender, adding the remaining vegetables during the last 30 minutes cooking time. Serve with mashed potatoes or boiled rice.

PIGEON BREASTS IN MUSHROOM AND TOMATO SAUCE
(4 small pigeons serve 4)

Remove the pigeon breasts from the bones. (Put bones into a saucepan with a bay leaf, salt, peppercorns, a clove of garlic and a few celery leaves. Cover with water, boil and then simmer to make stock). Turn the pigeon breasts in flour which has been seasoned with salt and pepper, then brown in 1 oz butter. Put pigeon breasts into a casserole. Strain stock, mix with 4 tbsps (4 x 15 ml spoons — 4 tbsps) tomato purée and pour over pigeon meat. Cook in a slow oven (300°F/150°C — mark 2) until tender—about 2½ hours, adding 4 oz (125 g — 4 oz) washed and chopped mushrooms during the last ten minutes or so. Sprinkle liberally with chopped parsley before serving.

POACHER'S STEW

Serves 6

Ingredients	Imperial	Metric	American
2 small rabbits jointed			
Flour, seasoned with salt and pepper	2 oz	50 gms	½ cup
Cooking fat	1½ oz	40 gms	3 tbsps
Pork sausages	½ lb	225 gms	½ lb
2 large onions chopped			
Tomato puree (optional)	3 tbsps	3 x 15 ml spoons	3 tbsps
Hot water	1 pint	575 ml	2½ cups
Tarragon and Basil (optional) each	¼ level tsp	¼ x 5 ml spoon	¼ tsp
Carrots, sliced ½″ thick (1¼ cm)	½ lb	225 gms	½ lb
Turnip diced	¼ lb	125 gms	¼ lb

All the cooking can be done in one pan, if you have the kind that can be used in the oven as well as on top of the stove — otherwise use a saucepan and then a casserole.

Turn rabbit portions in seasoned flour, to coat. Heat cooking fat in a large pan, brown the rabbit, then sausages and onion, transferring them from pan to casserole, as done. Sprinkle any remaining seasoned flour into the saucepan. Stir in tomato purée and hot water. Adjust seasoning, adding tarragon and basil if used, and bring to the boil. Pour this sauce over contents of casserole, add carrots and turnip. Cover casserole and cook in a very moderate oven (350°F/180°C — mark 4) for about 1½ hours or until rabbit is tender.

Serve with boiled rice or mashed potatoes.

ROAST CHICKEN WITH OATMEAL STUFFING

If you have never tried chicken or turkey stuffed with oatmeal (see stuffing recipe for "Beef Olives") and served with bread sauce (page 107) I advise you to do so now.

Choose a young, roasting chicken and, if frozen, allow to thaw completely. Stuff with the oatmeal stuffing (page 33) smear the bird with softened butter and cover breast with strips of streaky bacon. Parcel loosely in foil, joining edges together with a double fold on top and tucking in the énds. Place on a rack in a roasting tin and allow 30 minutes per lb (450 g or ½ kg — lb) in a moderately hot oven (400°F/200°C — mark 6). Remove foil and bacon during last 20 minutes to allow bird to brown. (If roasted without foil, prepare as above and cook for the same length of time but at 350°F/180°C — mark 4.)

PHEASANT AND MUSHROOM PIE

Serves 6

Ingredients	Imperial	Metric	American
1 plump pheasant (preferably a hen)			
Butter	1½ oz	40 gms	3 tbsps
Shallots, or baby onions peeled	8 oz	225 gms	8 oz
Mushrooms (wash, leave caps whole and dice stems)	12 oz	350 gms	12 oz
1 large carrot, finely diced			
Flour	1 oz	25 gms	3 tbsps
Good stock	¾ pint	425 ml	about 1¾ cups
Red wine	¼ pint	150 ml	10 tbsps
Redcurrant jelly	1 tbsp	1 x 15 ml spoon	1 tbsp
Lemon juice	1 tsp	1 x 5 ml spoon	1 tsp
2 strips lemon rind			
2 strips orange rind			
6 crushed juniper berries, if available			
Sprig chervil and parsley, if available			
Pinch of dried or fresh tarragon			
Puff pastry	8 oz	225 gms	8 oz
Beaten egg to glaze			

Brown pheasant well in butter, using a flame-proof casserole — or use a pan and transfer later to a casserole. Remove bird and saute shallots or onions, mushroom stems and carrot very gently in the same pan until they begin to change colour. (Reserve mushroom caps.) Return pheasant to the pan and add all remaining ingredients except, of course, the pastry and egg. Cover and cook in a very moderate oven (325°F/170°C — mark 3) for about 2 hours or until bird is very tender. Allow to cool, then joint bird, discarding skin and bones and leaving pheasant in reasonably large pieces.

Arrange pheasant, contents of casserole and mushroom caps in a large, deep pie dish. Cover with puff pastry, brush with egg and bake in a hot oven (435°F/225°C — mark 7) for 15 minutes or until pastry is well risen and deeply browned.

If made ahead of time, re-heat pie slowly in a very moderate oven (350°F/180°C — mark 4) for 20 to 30 minutes.

Serve with Forcemeat Balls and Braised Celery.

FORCEMEAT BALLS

For 12 balls:

Ingredients	Imperial	Metric	American
Shredded suet	2 oz	50 gms	⅜ cup
Fine soft breadcrumbs	4 oz	125 gms	2 cups
Finely chopped parsley	2 tbsps	2 x 15 ml spoons	2 tbsps
Salt and pepper			
Butter	1 oz	25 gms	2 tbsps
1 small chopped onion			
1 rasher lean bacon, chopped			
Enough beaten egg to bind			
To coat: Beaten egg and fine dry breadcrumbs			
Fat or oil to fry			

Combine suet, soft crumbs, parsley, and seasoning. Melt butter in a small pan and gently fry onion and bacon until softened. Mix with breadcrumb mixture and enough egg to bind and shape into small balls (about 1¼", 3 cm, diameter) using floured hands. Dip in beaten egg and coat balls in fine breadcrumbs.

Fry in either shallow or deep fat or oil until golden brown. Drain on crumpled paper towelling and keep warm.

N.B.   The forcemeat balls can be prepared and crumbed, ready for frying, ahead of time. Keep covered in a cool place or refrigerator.

BRAISED DUCKLING WITH ORANGE SAUCE

Allow one duckling (which weighs 5-6 lbs (2¼-2¾ kg) but there is a lot of bone) to serve 4.

Divide the duck into four portions, first cutting it into two equal halves with a length-wise split, then into quarters — each portion should have a piece of breast attached, there being two wing portions and two leg portions.

Melt 2 oz (50 g — ¼ cup) butter in a heavy pan and brown the duck all over, turning as necessary. Add ¼ pint (150 ml — 10 tbsps) stock made from the giblets and the juice of two oranges, plus 2-3 thin strips orange peel and a good dash of red wine. Cook in a moderately hot oven (400°F/200°C — mark 6) until very tender; lift duck pieces from the sauce onto a roasting tin and leave this in the oven, with the heat turned down while you finish the sauce. Strain liquid in which the duck was cooked into a bowl.

While the duck is cooking, in another pan melt 2 tbsps (2 x 15 ml spoons — 2 tbsps) butter and add 1 tbsp (1 x 15 ml spoon — 1 tbsp) each finely chopped shallots (or onion), celery and carrot and cook very gently until vegetables begin to change colour. Add 1 level tbsp (1 x 15 ml spoon — 1 tbsp) flour and stir over low heat until you have a deep brown paste. Withdraw from heat while you add 1 level tsp (1 x 5 ml spoon — 1 tsp) tomato purée and, gradually, ½ pint (275 ml — 1¼ cups) stock. Bring to the boil, stirring continuously until sauce thickens. Stir in the liquid in which the duck was cooked and a small glass of red wine. Simmer 5 minutes then strain into a clean pan, add 2 tbsps (2 x 15 ml spoons — 2 tbsps) red currant jelly and stir until it has dissolved. Add blanched strips of orange peel* and serve sauce separately.

Garnish duck with slices of fresh orange and watercress.

*To blanch, cut off thin strips of orange peel, using a vegetable parer, then cut them into very thin lengths, about an inch long. Cover these with cold water in a small pan, bring to the boil, then drain. Repeat this process twice with fresh cold water.

Egg, Savoury and Vegetable Dishes

The Scots are fond enough of egg and savoury dishes but vegetables are another matter! First-class vegetables can be and are grown in Scotland but treated most unimaginatively and, worse still, overcooked. (When my French, salad-loving mother first came to Scotland many years ago, she was taunted for eating "rabbits' food" but she did eventually convert her new friends and neighbours to the habit while they, in turn, introduced her to the delights of "drop scones" and "cloutie dumplings".)

SCOTCH EGGS

Ingredients	Imperial	Metric	American
4 small eggs, hard boiled (cooked for 12 minutes is ideal)			
Sausagemeat	1 lb	450 gms	1 lb
Flour to coat			
1 beaten egg			
Fine, dry breadcrumbs	4 oz	125 gms	2 cups
Oil or fat for deep frying			

Divide sausagemeat into four portions and flatten out each piece on a floured surface. Dip the cold, hard boiled eggs into flour before surrounding each completely with sausagemeat — make very sure there are no gaps in the meat. Dip in beaten egg, then coat thoroughly with breadcrumbs. Fry in very hot, deep oil or fat until golden brown (about 6 minutes), then drain on crumpled paper towelling. When cold, cut in two lengthwise and serve with salad and mayonnaise.

SMOKIE OMELETTE

One smokie is sufficient for 2 to 4 omelettes. Steam the smokie until well heated through, placing it in ¼" (¾ cm) or so of simmering hot water in a lidded pan. Remove flesh from the bones and discard skin and bones. Heat the omelette pan and melt a walnut of butter in it — pour in two beaten eggs per portion and, before the eggs set, scatter flaked smokie over them and season with pepper. (No salt is necessary.) Fold the omelette over, slide it onto a warm plate and serve immediately.

SCOTCH WOODCOCK

There is a game bird called woodcock but the prefix "Scotch" before woodcock indicates the following savoury — I have never been able to discover why.

Ingredients	Imperial	Metric	American
1 small tin anchovies			
A little freshly ground black pepper or a dash of cayenne			
3 egg yolks			
Cream or top of the milk	3 tbsps	3 x 15 ml spoons	3 tbsps
Four 2" (5 cm) fingers or rounds of hot, buttered toast			

Drain the anchovies and pound them to a paste, adding a good dash of pepper. Beat the egg yolks and stir them into the cream in a small, thick pan. Heat gently, stirring continuously, until thick and creamy, being careful not to let the mixture boil or it may curdle. Spread the hot, buttered toast with the anchovy paste and pour the egg mixture over each. Garnish with chopped parsley and serve very hot.

FRIED AND BUTTERED CABBAGE

I first tasted this on the Isle of Barra and it is very good — although I very much doubt that it is Scottish in origin.

Shred some white, winter cabbage very finely — it should be sliced as thinly as it possibly can be, using a very sharp knife. Treat a small onion in the same way. Fry both vegetables together very gently indeed, in a little butter, until just softened and season well with salt and pepper.

MISS THORA'S KALE SPREAD

This is an Orkney recipe — or, at least, it is the invention of an Orcadian lady — and I think it very original and a most appetising, savoury spread for buttered baps, water biscuits or oatcakes.

Finely shred some curly kale and mix with an equal quantity (when combined) of chopped parsley and chives. Bind with thick mayonnaise.

GREEN CURLY KALE

"Kale" is how this vegetable is spelled on the seed packets (strangely enough, I have never found kale on sale at the greengrocers in Scotland and it is accepted that one must grow one's own, although it is such a widely used vegetable and an essential ingredient of real Scotch broth). The old Scots spelling, however, seems to have been "kail".

To cook kale as a vegetable, trim away the thick, centre stalks and chop the leaves roughly. Just cover them with water in a large pan, bring to the boil, then drain very thoroughly, squeezing to extract as much water as possible. Chop again, this time very finely, and return the kale to the pan. Sprinkle lightly with a level tbsp (1 x 15 ml spoon — 1 tbsp) or so of oatmeal (optional), season with salt and pepper and toss with a knob of butter. Cover and leave the pan on the side of the stove or over very gentle heat for 10 minutes before serving.

BLACK OR WHITE PUDDINGS

These were certainly sold by street criers in Edinburgh as early as the 15th century — perhaps earlier.

These are on sale at any Scottish butcher's shop and seldom, if ever, now made at home — although I have done so, using old Auntie Nan's "white pudding stuffer" — a large, funnel-like piece of equipment through which the pudding ingredients are stuffed into skins. White puddings are made with oatmeal, onion, shredded suet, salt and pepper (much the same as oatmeal stuffing, page 33) and put into skins, like large sausages. They are usually boiled gently, then browned in a frying pan — or they can be dipped in batter and deep fried — and served nowadays with chip potatoes.

Black puddings are made from the same ingredients as white, but mixed with ox or pig's blood. They come in large, sausage shapes — about 2″ (5 cm) in diameter — and are then sliced ½″ (1¼ cm) thick and fried, before being served for breakfast or "high tea", as part of a mixed grill.

SKIRLIES

This is another oatmeal and onion dish. Originally, skirlies were made by sizzling some chopped suet in a frying pan until it melted, then adding chopped onion and enough oatmeal to absorb the fat. After 5-10 minutes the mixture would be thoroughly cooked, then it would be seasoned well with salt and pepper and served with boiled potatoes. More recently, skirlies have come to mean this same oatmeal mixture enclosed in pastry, so that they can be heated, like pies, in the oven.

CLAPSHOT (An Orkney dish)

For this you need an equal quantity of boiled potatoes and turnip — cut the turnip into large dice and put it on to boil first, in salted water. Cut the potatoes into pieces roughly equal in size and add to the turnip. When done, drain and mash together. Stir in a small, grated or finely chopped onion and a pat of butter or a tbsp or two of cream — enough to make a smooth consistency. Season with salt and pepper and sprinkle with snipped chives, when available.

BRAISED CELERY

Serves 8

Ingredients	*Imperial*	*Metric*	*American*
2 large heads celery			
Butter	**2 oz**	**50 gms**	**¼ cup**
Chicken stock (1 cube) or tinned consomme	**½ pint**	**275 ml**	**2¼ cups**

Wash and trim the celery of its larger leaves, then cut into 4" (10 cm) pieces. Melt butter in a fairly large pan and add celery, turning it gently, for 3 minutes. Turn into an oven dish or casserole, pour over stock and cover dish with foil or lid. Cook in a moderate oven (350°F/180°C — mark 4) or in a moderately hot oven (400°F/200°C — mark 6) until tender — takes about 1 hour at the lower temperature or 45 minutes at the higher.

STOVIES

There are many different versions of this old Scottish recipe, e.g. leftover beef or lamb and gravy can be added to make a substantial main course. Use unblemished potatoes of about the same size — they can be old or new.

Ingredients	*Imperial*	*Metric*	*American*
Dripping	**1½ oz**	**40 gms**	**3 tbsps**
2 medium sized onions, sliced			
Potatoes (peeled)	**1½ lbs**	**675 gms**	**1½ lbs**
Hot water			
Salt			
Fine ground oatmeal (optional)			

Melt dripping in a medium sized saucepan and fry the sliced onions until golden. Add potatoes, sliced about ⅜ths" (2 cm) thick, to the pan and pour in enough water to come half way up the pan. Sprinkle with salt, bring to the boil, cover and simmer very gently until potatoes are done. Shake a handful of oatmeal over potatoes, replace lid and shake pan well. Leave covered on side of stove for 10 minutes before serving.

COLCANNON

This makes a tasty dish for supper or high tea. It is very similar to the English "Bubble and Squeak".

Ingredients	Imperial	Metric	American
Dripping	1 oz	25 gms	2 tbsps
2 cups chopped cooked cabbage (teacups or measuring cups)			
2 cups cold mashed potatoes (teacups or measuring cups)			
1 small onion, chopped			
Salt and pepper to taste			
4 eggs			

Melt the dripping in a frying pan and toss the cabbage and potatoes together in the pan until well heated through; season to taste. Place in a buttered, fireproof dish and bake in a pre-heated, moderately hot oven (400°F/200°C — mark 6) for 20 minutes or so, until nicely browned. Serve a poached or fried egg on top of each portion.

Hot Puddings and Cold Desserts

The Scottish sweet-tooth is well known and no meal is considered worthy of guests without a pudding or cakes, for "afters". Visitors to Scotland will soon notice that it is a national custom to pour custard — or even milk — over most pies and "everyday" puddings such as crumbles, steamed puddings, baked sponges — a habit to which I do not personally ascribe. To me, it seems such a waste to take the trouble to create crisp, golden pastry only to reduce it to sogginess within seconds, in a sea of custard — but I cannot find anyone (and certainly none in my own family) who agrees with me.

AUNTIE NAN'S "CLOUTIE DUMPLING"

The pudding is boiled in a floured cloth, (or "cloutie") for that authentic "flattened ball" appearance but you can, of course, cook it in the usual buttered bowl if you don't feel like trying the old way.

Ingredients	Imperial	Metric	American
Plain flour	8 oz	225 gms	2 cups
Cinnamon	1 level tsp	1 x 5 ml spoon	1 tsp
Mixed spice	1 level tsp	1 x 5 ml spoon	1 tsp
Baking soda	1 level tsp	1 x 5 ml spoon	1 tsp
Sugar	8 oz	225 gms	1 cup
Shredded suet	4 oz	125 gms	¾ cup
Mixed dried fruit	8 oz	225 gms	1½ cups
About 1 teacupful milk, to mix			

Sift flour, spices and soda into a large bowl. Add sugar, suet and fruit and mix to a soft dropping consistency with the milk. Wring out a large square of clean cotton or linen cloth in very hot water. Spread out, dust cloth liberally with flour. Spoon pudding mixture into the centre. Gather up the ends of the cloth and tie tightly, close to the pudding, with string.

Put an upturned plate in a large saucepan, set pudding on top of the plate and pour in boiling water to come three quarters of the way up the pudding. Simmer steadily for 2½ hours.

This pudding can be made ahead of time, in which case store it as follows. First, hang it above a plate or basin until it stops dripping. When it is cold, remove cloth and replace it with a fresh, dry one. Store in a cool place and re-boil for 2 hours before serving.

RAISIN AND SPICED BREAD PUDDING

Ingredients	Imperial	Metric	American
Stale bread (4 large slices)	4 oz	125 gms	
Milk	¾ pint	425 ml	scant 2 cups
Raisins	2 oz	50 gms	⅜ cup
Sugar	4 oz	125 gms	½ cup
Mixed spice	1½ tsps	1½ x 5 ml spoons	1½ tsps
Knob of butter			

Break the bread into a saucepan; add milk, raisins, sugar and mixed spice and bring to the boil; stir and simmer for a few minutes until the mixture is well pulped. Add a knob of butter, stir until melted and turn the pudding into a buttered baking dish or casserole. Bake in a pre-heated, moderate oven (375°F/190°C — mark 5) for 30 minutes, until slightly crisp on top. Serve hot.

DAMSON CRUMBLE

Ingredients	Imperial	Metric	American
Damsons	1 lb	450 gms	1 lb
Sugar	4 oz	125 gms	½ cup
Water	5 tbsps	5 x 15 ml spoons	5 tbsps
Flour	6 oz	175 gms	¾ cup
Brown sugar	3 oz	75 gms	⅜ cup
Ginger	1 level tsp	1 x 5 ml spoon	1 tsp
Margarine	2 oz	50 gms	¼ cup

Stone damsons and stew gently in sugar and water until just softened. Turn into a deep ovenproof dish or pie plate. Mix flour, brown sugar and ginger together and rub in margarine. Sprinkle crumble mixture over fruit and lightly level top. Bake in a moderate oven (375°F/190°C — mark 5) until crumble top is nicely browned and the fruit beginning to bubble through — about 30 minutes.

PLUM CHARLOTTE

Ingredients	Imperial	Metric	American
Plums	1½ lbs	675 gms	1½ lbs
Sugar, depending on sweetness of fruit	4-8 oz	125-225 gms	½-1 cup
Cinnamon	¼ level tsp	¼ x 5 ml spoon	¼ tsp
Water	½ cup	125 ml	½ cup
6 thin slices white bread, crusts removed			
Butter, melted	4 oz	125 gms	½ cup

Stew plums with sugar, cinnamon and water until just tender, taking care that they do not become pulpy. Set aside to cool.

Cut a small circle of bread to fit the base of a 1½ pint (850 ml — 3¾ cup) clear, heatproof bowl and another circle to fit the top. Completely line the bowl with strips of the remaining bread, first dipping each piece in melted butter. Remove stones from the plums and pour into the lined dish. Cover fruit with the piece of bread cut to fit the top of the bowl and previously dipped in butter.

Bake in a moderate oven (375°F/190°C — mark 5) for about 1 hour or until you can see that the bread is toasted golden brown. Serve in the bowl or cool slightly before turning onto a serving dish.

APPLE AND BRAMBLE PIE

Brambles (or Blackberries) have their brief season in September — combine them with apples and spice them with cinnamon in this delectable fruit pie. (Make a rhubarb pie in the same way, substituting ginger for cinnamon).

Serves 6

Ingredients	Imperial	Metric	American
Short crust pastry — make from:			
Plain flour	**6 oz**	**175 gms**	**1½ cups**
Butter and/or lard,	**4 oz**	**125 gms**	**½ cup**
(or use 1 large pkt frozen pastry)			
Filling:			
Prepared weight of fruit — use any	**1½ lbs**	**675 gms**	**1½ lbs**
proportion of peeled, cored and			
sliced apples with washed			
blackberries			
Sugar	**6 oz**	**175 gms**	**¾ cup**
Flour (+ cinnamon to taste)	**2 level tbsps**	**2 x 15 ml spoons**	**2 tbsps**
Butter	**½ oz**	**15 gms**	**1 tbsp**
A little milk, to glaze			
Sifted icing sugar, to finish			
(optional)			

Roll out pastry thinly on a floured surface. Use a little more than half to line a buttered pie plate, 8-9″ (20-22 cm) in diameter and at least 1″ (2½ cm) deep. From the rest of the pastry, cut a lid which will overlap the pie plate by about 1″ (2½ cm) all round and set this aside.

Arrange the fruit in the lined pie plate. Mix sugar, flour and cinnamon together and spoon over the fruit. Dot with tiny pieces of butter.

Moisten pastry lid with cold water and set, moistened side down, on top of the pie. Seal to bottom layer of pastry by pressing edges together. Trim and flute the edge and cut three small slits in the centre of the pie to allow steam to escape. Brush top with milk. Bake in a moderately hot oven (400°F/200°C — mark 6) until golden brown — the fruit should be tender when tested with a fork and have begun to bubble through the slits.

Serve warm, with custard or pouring cream.

APPLE SYRUP DUMPLING

Ingredients	*Imperial*	*Metric*	*American*
Plain flour)	**10 oz**	**275 gms**	**2½ cups**
Baking soda) or use self-raising) flour	**½ tsp**	**½ x 5 ml spoon**	**½ tsp**
Cream of tartar)	**1 tsp**	**1 x 5 ml spoon**	**1 tsp**
Pinch of salt			
Margarine	**4 oz**	**125 gms**	**½ cup**
A little milk or cold water			
Cooking apples (not too hard a variety)	**1 lb**	**500 gms**	**1 lb**
Currants	**2 oz**	**50 gms**	**⅜ cup**
Cinnamon	**¼ tsp**	**¼ x 5 ml spoon**	**¼ tsp**
Ginger	**¼ tsp**	**¼ x 5 ml spoon**	**¼ tsp**

Half of a one pound tin (½ kg) of golden syrup (more if you like a very sweet dumpling)

Sift flour, soda, cream of tartar and salt into a large mixing bowl and rub in the margarine; add just enough milk or water to make a firm dough. Turn onto a floured surface and lightly roll two-thirds of the paste to about ¼″ (¾ cm) thick; ease this carefully into a buttered, 1½ pint (850 ml — 3¾ cup) pudding basin; roll out the remaining paste to make a round for the top of the basin and set it aside.

Peel and slice the apples fairly thinly and fill up the pudding basin with layers of sliced apple, currants, spice and syrup, in that order; put on the lid of paste and pinch the edges together to seal well; cover with tinfoil or a cloth, securely tied with string round the rim.

Steam for 2½ hours, replenishing the hot water as necessary. To serve, either turn the dumpling out onto a dish or serve in the pudding basin, with a napkin folded round it.

JAM ROLY POLY

This was the one and only dish that could be guaranteed to bring my father in promptly from the garden — even with a high wind buffeting his prize chrysanthemums!

Ingredients	*Imperial*	*Metric*	*American*
Plain flour) or self-raising	**8 oz**	**225 gms**	**2 cups**
Baking Powder) flour	**2 tsps**	**2 x 5 ml spoons**	**2 tsps**
Pinch of salt			
Shredded suet	**4 oz**	**125 gms**	**¾ cup**
Cold water roughly	**¼ pint**	**150 ml**	**10 tbsps**
Raspberry or strawberry jam about	**½ lb**	**225 gms**	**1 cup**
A little caster sugar			

Sift flour, baking powder and salt into a mixing bowl and mix thoroughly with the shredded suet; add just enough water to make a pliable but firm dough; turn onto a floured surface and roll out to an oblong about ¼" (¾ cm) thick. Brush the edges with cold water and spread with jam, leaving an inch of margin all round. Roll up and seal the ends by pinching well together; dust with flour. Rinse out a cloth (about the size of a large table napkin) in hot water, wring it out well and dust thickly with flour. Roll up the pudding in the cloth, tie the ends, leaving room for the pudding to swell.

Invert a plate on the bottom of a large saucepan, put in the pudding and cover with boiling water. Boil for 2½-3 hours. (Do not move or turn the pudding at all while it is cooking). Lift out the pudding, untie and unroll the cloth. Dust the pudding with caster sugar, place it in a warm oven (325°F/170°C — mark 3) for 5 minutes to dry out slightly.

Serve hot, with a custard sauce.

BREAD AND BUTTER PUDDING

Butter 6 slices of white bread, remove the crusts and cut each slice in half diagonally. Arrange the triangles of bread in a buttered,1½-2 pint (1 litre — 5 cup) baking dish. Sprinkle 2 oz (50 g — ⅜ cup) raisins or sultanas between and around the bread.

Warm ¾ pint (425 ml — 2 cups) milk and 2 oz (50 g — ¼ cup) sugar together in a saucepan, stirring until sugar dissolves. Add to this 2 beaten eggs and ¼ tsp (¼ x 5 ml — ¼ tsp) vanilla essence. Pour egg and milk mixture over the bread and bake in a moderate oven (375°F/190°C — mark 5) until set and golden. In Scotland, a jug of milk accompanies this and all similar puddings to the table and each person will pour some around his or her portion of pudding.

CRANACHAN (A Highland dish, served on special occasions)

This is a combination of lightly whipped cream, toasted oatmeal, honey (or sugar) and whisky (or Drambuie) in whatever proportions you find most pleasing. I suggest the following, for 4 servings.

Ingredients	Imperial	Metric	American
Double cream	½ pint	275 ml	1¼ cups
Oatmeal which has been toasted until crisp and lightly browned in the oven	4 level tbsps	4 x 15 ml spoons	4 tbsps
Whisky or Drambuie	3 tbsps	3 x 15 ml spoons	3 tbsps
Clear honey — clover honey is good, heather honey even better	3 tbsps	3 x 15 ml spoons	3 tbsps

Whip the cream until thick but not stiff, then fold in the remaining ingredients and spoon into individual dishes. Keep cool until serving time — but it should not be too chilly.

ORKNEY PANCAKES

This is an original and absolutely delicious recipe which the Misses Bain of Kirkwall created when they were asked to recommend a special Orcadian dessert for a dinner featuring Orkney food. The occasion was a National Farmers' Union dinner for several hundred guests at Aviemore and, said Mary Bain, "I didn't know what to suggest until I suddenly thought of Norman Firth's cough mixture." (My mind boggled for a moment, until it was explained that the "cough mixture" was, in fact, a blend of honey and whisky!) To this throat-soothing mixture they added a pinch of salt and thick Orkney cream, as a filling for the ultra-thin pancakes they had enjoyed on holiday in Iceland.

Makes about 20 pancakes. Serves 6 to 8.

Ingredients	Imperial	Metric	American
Batter:			
1 egg			
Caster sugar	1 level tbsp	1 x 15 ml spoon	1 tbsp
Plain flour	4 oz	125 gms	1 cup
Salt	¼ level tsp	¼ x 15 ml spoon	¼ tsp
Baking soda	½ level tsp	½ x 5 ml spoon	½ tsp
Melted butter	1 tbsp	1 x 15 ml spoon	1 tbsp
Vanilla essence	¼ tsp	¼ x 15 ml spoon	¼ tsp
Milk	16 fl oz	450 ml	2 cups
Filling:			
Heather honey	3 tbsps	3 x 15 ml spoons	3 tbsps
Malt whisky	1½ tbsps	1½ x 15 ml spoons	1½ tbsps
Pinch salt			
Double cream	¼ pint	150 ml	10 tbsps

Beat egg and sugar together and transfer to a large bowl. Mix and sift flour, salt and baking soda together. Stir half of the flour mixture into the egg and sugar. Stir in melted butter and vanilla, then remaining flour. Thin gradually with the milk and beat smooth — the batter will be very thin.

Slowly heat a small frying pan or omelette pan, which should be very hot before you start to cook the pancakes. Lightly grease the pan and pour in just enough batter to coat the base, tilting pan slightly forward and back to complete the coating fairly quickly and evenly. When browned on one side (you will see the edges becoming coloured) turn and cook on the other side. The second side cooks very quickly. Stack pancakes as they are made in a warm place, wrapped in a tea towel, if you are going to use them immediately afterwards — otherwise, separate each pancake with a square of lightly oiled, greaseproof paper as you stack them, then wrap in foil, ready to warm later in the oven.

Make filling an hour or so ahead of time and keep chilled. Stir honey, whisky and salt together to blend thoroughly. Whip cream until quite thick, then fold gently into the honey/whisky.

Just before serving, place a dessertspoonful of filling on each pancake and either roll up or fold each into four.

SCOTCH TRIFLE

This traditional Scottish pudding has changed considerably over the years and now often includes jelly, set with fruit (usually sliced bananas or chopped, tinned fruit.) The following is a more or less traditional version. Split stale sponge cake(s) and spread with raspberry jam. Slice and set in a glass dish. Sprinkle sherry over the sponge — it should be quite soggy. Top with rich custard, then sweetened, vanilla flavoured whipped cream. Decorate with glacé cherries and chopped walnuts.

APPLE SPONGE PUDDING

Ingredients	Imperial	Metric	American
3 medium sized cooking apples			
Powdered ginger	½ tsp	½ x 5 ml spoon	½ tsp
Golden syrup	4 tbsps	4 x 15 ml spoons	4 tbsps
Margarine	2 oz	50 gms	¼ cup
Sugar	4 oz	125 gms	½ cup
1 egg			
1 teacup plain flour			
Baking powder	1 tsp	1 x 5 ml spoon	1 tsp
¼ teacup Milk	2 fl oz	50 ml	¼ cup
Lemon juice	¼ tsp	¼ x 5 ml spoon	¼ tsp

Peel, core and slice apples thinly; grease an 8″ (20 cm) pie plate or 2 pint (1 litre — 3¾ cup) casserole, put in the apples, sprinkle with powdered ginger and top with golden syrup. Cream margarine and sugar, add the eggs, then stir in the sifted, self-raising flour; thin with the milk and flavour with the lemon juice. Pour sponge mixture over the apples and bake in a pre-heated, moderate oven (375°F/190°C — mark 5) for 35-40 minutes or until sponge tests done, i.e. when a thin stick or skewer comes out clean when inserted in the centre of the sponge.

Serve warm, with cream or a cooled, creamy custard.

PLUM CRUMBLE

Halve and stone 1 lb (450 g — 1 lb) plums and put into a 1½-2 pint (1 litre — 5 cup) oven dish. Strew generously with sugar, to taste.

For the crumble topping, rub 2 oz (50 g — ¼ cup) margarine or butter into 4 oz (125 g — ½ cup) flour, sifted with 1 level tsp (1 x 15 ml spoon — 1 tsp) cinnamon. Stir in 2 oz (50 g — ¼ cup) soft brown sugar and spoon mixture over plums. Bake in a moderate oven (375°F/190°C — mark 5) until browned and bubbly — about 35 minutes.

GINGER SPONGE PUDDING

Serves 4-6

Use a 1½ pint (850 ml — 3¾ cup) mould or pudding basin.

Ingredients	Imperial	Metric	American
Margarine	2 oz	50 gms	¼ cup
Sugar	2 oz	50 gms	¼ cup
Egg	1	1	1
Syrup	1 tbsp	1 x 15 ml spoon	1 tbsp
Flour, self-raising*	4 oz	125 gms	½ cup
Powdered ginger	1 level tsp	1 x 5 ml spoon	1 tsp
Baking soda	¼ level tsp	¼ x 5 ml spoon	¼ tsp
Milk	4 tbsps	4 x 15 ml spoons	4 tbsps

Beat margarine and sugar together until creamy. Add the well beaten egg and the syrup. Mix thoroughly. Sift flour (*add ½ level tsp baking powder, if using plain flour) and ginger together and gradually beat into the mixture. Dissolve the baking soda in the milk and stir into mixture. Pour into the well buttered mould or pudding basin, cover securely with lid, foil or buttered paper and place in a large saucepan, with boiling water coming half-way up the basin. Steam for 1½ hours, replenishing the hot water as necessary.

Turn the pudding onto a serving dish and accompany with a sauceboat of warmed golden syrup or with a creamy custard.

For a change —
Use the same basic recipe but —
1. Add a few chopped dates or some mincemeat or dried fruit.
2. Omit ginger and put 3 tbsps (3 x 15 ml spoons — 3 tbsps) jam in the base of the bowl.
3. Omit ginger and add 2 level tbsps (2 x 15 ml spoons — 2 tbsps) cocoa powder to dry ingredients.

GRANDMAMA'S PLUM PUDDING

Unusual (like Grandmama!) and very, very good.

Makes 3 puddings.

Ingredients	Imperial	Metric	American
Dates finely chopped	1 lb	450 gms	1 lb
Seedless raisins	1 lb	450 gms	1 lb
Sultanas	1 lb	450 gms	1 lb
Chopped mixed peel	4 oz	125 gms	¾ cup
Butter or margarine	1 lb	450 gms	2 cups
Brown sugar	1 lb	450 gms	1 lb
5 eggs			
Golden syrup	4 oz	125 ml	4 tbsps
Grated rind and juice of 1 lemon			
Self-raising flour OR	6 oz	175 gms	1½ cups
Plain flour + Baking powder			
(Baking powder	¾ level tsp	¾ x 5 ml spoons	¾ tsp)
Mixed spice and nutmeg each	1 level tsp	1 x 5 ml spoon	1 tsp
Ground almonds	1 level tbsp	1 x 15 ml spoon	1 tbsp
Fresh brown breadcrumbs	1 lb	½ kg	8 cups
1 wineglass rum or brandy			
Milk to mix	3-4 tbsps	3-4 x 15 ml spoons	3-4 tbsps

Mix prepared fruit together. Cream butter and margarine with brown sugar until fluffy. Beat eggs in well. Stir in syrup, rind and lemon juice. Mix in flour, sifted with spices. Add almonds, breadcrumbs, fruit and peel. Add rum or brandy and milk, to blend. Cover and let stand overnight.

Well butter three two-pint (1 litre — 5 cup) pudding basins, place round of buttered greaseproof paper in each. Divide mixture among basins, cover with two thicknesses of buttered greaseproof paper and a pudding cloth — or with foil. Tie securely round the rim leaving room for pudding to expand.

Steam at least six hours, with boiling water coming half way up the basins, in covered pans. Remove wet coverings from puddings when cold and replace with dry ones before storing in a cool place. Before serving, steam again for 2-3 hours.

HEATHER HONEY SUNDAE (A more modern Scottish dessert)

Put scoops of vanilla ice cream into individual glass dishes. Drizzle clear, warmed heather honey over the ice cream and scatter with chopped walnuts.

BLACKCURRANT TOFFEE PUDDING

Has a chewy topping and bubbly fruit filling.

Ingredients	Imperial	Metric	American
Blackcurrants	1 lb	450 gms	1 lb
Sugar	4 oz	125 gms	½ cup
Cinnamon (optional)	¼ level tsp	¼ x 5 ml spoon	¼ tsp
Fine white breadcrumbs	3 oz	75 gms	1½ cups
Soft brown sugar	4 oz	125 gms	½ cup
Shredded suet	1 oz	25 gms	2 tbsps

Put washed currants, with stalks removed, into a buttered 2-pint (1 litre) oven dish. Mix together sugar and cinnamon, if used, and fork into blackcurrants.

Mix breadcrumbs, soft brown sugar and suet together and pile evenly on top of fruit.

Place near the top of a hot oven (450°F/230°C — mark 8) for 15 minutes. Reduce heat to 350°F/180°C — mark 4 for a further 15 minutes. The top of the pudding should be deeply browned.

Serve with pouring cream or custard.

STRAWBERRY MACAROON TRIFLE

Ingredients	Imperial	Metric	American
Sugar	4 oz	125 gms	½ cup
Water	4 tbsps	4 x 15 ml spoons	4 tbsps
Thinly pared strip lemon peel			
Double cream	¼ pint	150 ml	10 tbsps
Single cream	2½ fl oz	5 x 15 ml spoons	5 tbsps
Strawberries	about ¾ lb	350 gms	¾ lb
Sifted icing sugar	2 oz	50 gms	¼ cup
Small Macaroon biscuits	4 oz	125 gms	4 oz

Place sugar, water and lemon rind in a small thick pan. Stir over low heat until sugar dissolves, then simmer gently for 1-2 minutes. Strain and allow syrup to cool. Combine creams and sugar syrup and whisk together until thick. Toss strawberries with icing sugar and crush lightly with a fork.

Reserve 4 macaroons for decoration. Place a layer of macaroons in the base of a glass serving dish (or in individual dishes), then a layer of crushed strawberries, then a layer of cream. Repeat layers once more. Crush the reserved macaroons and sprinkle on top.

DRAMBUIE SOUFFLÉ

This is my own contribution to the repertoire of "special occasion" Scottish desserts.

Serves 6/8

Ingredients	Imperial	Metric	American
Milk	¾ pint	425 ml	2 scant cups
4 standard eggs (separated)			
Caster sugar	3 oz	75 gms	⅓ cup
1 envelope Gelatin	3 level tsps	3 x 5 ml spoons	3 tsps
Cold water	5 tbsps	5 x 15 ml spoons	5 tbsps
1 miniature bottle Drambuie			
Double cream	½ pint	275 ml	1¼ cups
Almond macaroon biscuits	4 oz	125 gms	4 oz
To decorate — flaked almonds, toasted in the oven	1 oz	25 gms	1 tbsp

Heat milk gradually to just under boiling point. Beat egg yolks with the sugar, using an electric or rotary whisk, until thick and pale. Pour the hot milk, in a thin stream, into the beaten eggs and sugar, whisking as you pour. Return to the saucepan and cook gently, stirring continuously, until the custard thickens slightly. Draw away from heat.

Sprinkle gelatin over the cold water in a cup. Set cup in a pan of hot water and stir until gelatin dissolves. Stir into custard along with one third of the Drambuie liqueur. Set custard over ice while you whip the cream until thick but not too stiff, and very stiffly whisk the egg whites. Prepare a soufflé dish, using a six inch (15 cm) diameter, No.2 size. Tie a double thickness of greaseproof paper or a single thickness of foil, 2" wider than the depth of the dish, round the outside rim of the dish very firmly. (When the soufflé is set and this "collar" peeled away, the soufflé will project over the rim of the dish). Set an oiled, 1 lb (½ kg) jam jar in the centre.

When the custard mixture, which should be stirred occasionally, is on the point of setting, fold in first about two thirds of the whipped cream (reserving the remainder for decoration) and then the egg whites. Pour into the soufflé dish, around the jam jar, and leave to set in a cool place. Break up the macaroon biscuits, sprinkle them with the remaining liqueur and leave in a cool place too.*

An hour or so before serving, carefully ease out the jam jar and peel off the collar from the soufflé. Spoon the liqueur-soaked macaroons into the centre cavity. Stiffly whip the reserved whipped cream and spoon some on top of the macaroons, if necessary, to level the top. Spread a thin layer of cream over the top surface, pipe loops around the edge — using a large star nozzle in a forcing bag. Insert a toasted almond between each loop.

*N.B. The soufflé can be prepared and left to set the date before serving, up to this point.

RASPBERRY PLATE TART

Line a shallow pie plate — about 7" (18 cm) diameter — with short pastry. Fill with fresh raspberries and strew liberally with caster sugar, using about 4 oz (125 gms — ½ cup) sugar to 12 oz (350 gms — 12 oz) raspberries. Top with a pastry lid, having moistened the underneath edge with cold water, and pinch edges together to seal well. Make 2-3 small slits in the top. Brush with milk and bake in a moderate oven for about 35 minutes, until pastry is browned and the filling begins to bubble through the slits. Take from the oven and sprinkle with caster or sifted icing sugar. Best served warm, with cream.

FROZEN RHUBARB PUDDING

Rhubarb grows rampant in Scottish gardens and I am continually devising new ways of using it — this one has proved very popular.

Serves 6.

Ingredients	Imperial	Metric	American
Biscuit shell:			
Digestive biscuits or ginger biscuits	6 oz	175 gms	6 oz
Melted butter	3 oz	75 gms	6 tbsps
Caster sugar	3 level tbsps	3 x 15 ml spoons	3 tbsps
Filling:			
Sweetened rhubarb puree Approx	½ pint	275 ml	1¼ cups
Stew rhubarb with water and	½ lb	225 gms	½ lb
sweetening and then puree in a			
liquidiser or by pressing through a			
wire sieve or mouli mill.			
1 small tin condensed milk			
Double cream	¼ pint	150 ml	10 tbsps

Crush biscuits into fine crumbs (easiest way is to put biscuits into a stout paper bag and bash with a rolling pin). Combine crumbs with melted butter and the sugar. Press firmly into base and sides of a 8-9" (20-22 cm) shallow pie plate. Leave to chill while you prepare the filling.

Cool the rhubarb purée and fold in the condensed milk. Lightly whip the cream and fold half of it into the fruit mixture, which then turn into the crumb shell. Freeze until firm. Whip remaining cream stiff enough to pipe round the edge of the dish, before serving.

To freeze — if it is intended to store this in the deep freeze, first line your pie plate with foil. Remove pie plate when frozen and wrap dessert in polythene or foil. (Whipped cream decoration can be added before or after freezing but preferably just before serving.) Keeps up to 2 months.

GOOSEBERRY SORBET

This refreshing, fruit-and-water ice is out of the ordinary, easy to make and quite inexpensive — other fruits can be substituted in the same recipe.

Serves 8.

Ingredients	*Imperial*	*Metric*	*American*
Green gooseberries	**1 lb**	**450 gms**	**1 lb**
Water	**6 tbsps**	**6 x 15 ml spoons**	**6 tbsps**
Sugar	**4 oz**	**125 gms**	**½ cup**
Sugar syrup — Sugar +¼ pint water			
Sugar	**4 oz**	**125 gms**	**½ cup**
2 egg whites			

Top and tail gooseberries and cook them gently with the 6 tbsps (6 x 15 ml spoons — 6 tbsps) water and 4 oz (125 gms — ½ cup) sugar until soft. Meanwhile, boil sugar syrup ingredients together in a small pan for 5 minutes. Purée the gooseberries in an electric liquidiser or by pressing through a wire sieve, combine with the sugar syrup and leave to cool. Turn into ice trays and freeze until mushy — about 45 minutes at coldest setting. Empty into a large, chilled bowl, break up and beat smooth. Fold in stiffly beaten egg whites. Return mixture to ice trays and freeze until firm.

Transfer to ordinary refrigeration about 1 hour before serving.

SOFT FRUIT ICE CREAMS

Raspberry and Strawberry Ice Cream

Combine ½ pint (275 ml — 1¼ cups) fruit purée (strained, if you prefer, and sweetened to taste) with 1 small tin condensed milk. Fold in ¼ pint (150 ml — 10 tbsps) double cream, lightly whipped, and then one stiffly beaten egg white. Freeze until firm.

Remove to ordinary refrigeration half an hour or so before serving.

Gooseberry, Blackcurrant, Bramble, Rhubarb Ice Cream

First make a sugar syrup, using 4 oz (125 gms — ½ cup) sugar to ½ pint (275 ml — 1¼ cups) water and boiling together for 3 minutes. Soften fruit by stewing it gently in this syrup before proceeding as above.

Freezer storage — up to six months.

SOFT FRUIT FOOL

Useful for using up small pickings of a variety of fruits — and the combination is absolutely delicious.

Serves 6.

Ingredients	Imperial	Metric	American
1 lb mixed soft fruits, e.g.:			
Blackcurrants	2 oz	50 gms	2 oz
Redcurrants	2 oz	50 gms	2 oz
Cherries (stoned)	4 oz	125 gms	4 oz
Raspberries	4 oz	125 gms	4 oz
Strawberries	4 oz	125 gms	4 oz
Sugar	4 oz	125 gms	½ cup
Double cream	¼ pint	150 ml	10 tbsps
Single cream	2½ fl oz	5 x 15 ml spoons	5 tbsps

Stew firmer fruits, such as blackcurrants, redcurrants and cherries, very gently until tender with sugar, using 1 oz (25 gms — 2 tbsps) sugar to each ¼ lb (150 gms — 4 oz) fruit. Stew raspberries and strawberries with the same proportion of sugar and crush with a fork. Press all the sugared fruit through a wire sieve or blend to a purée in an electric liquidiser. Whip creams together until thick but not too stiff and fold into fruit, reserving some of the cream, if liked to pipe for decoration. Turn fruit fool into individual glass dishes and leave in a cool place and decorate before serving with a little whipped cream, if you have kept some in reserve, on top of each.

Note: The above recipe can be frozen to make very good ice cream — the addition of two stiffly beaten egg whites, folded in last, will make it go further and improve the texture.

FRESH REDCURRANT JELLY

Wash and de-stalk 1 lb redcurrants (you will find de-stalking much quicker if you use a fork), setting aside 4 good sprigs for decoration. Simmer fruit gently with 4 oz (125 gms — ½ cup) sugar (loaf sugar, for preference) and ½ pint (275 ml — 1¼ cups) water until sugar dissolves — about 5 minutes. Strain through a piece of muslin placed over a sieve or through a jelly bag.*

Dissolve 3 level tsps (3 x 5 ml spoons — 3 tsps) Gelatin in the juice of 1 large lemon, as previously described, and stir into the redcurrant juice. If necessary, make up to 1 pint (575 ml — 2½ cups) with water.

Pour into a wetted, 1 pint (575 ml — 2½ cup) mould and leave to set. Before serving, unmould and decorate the base, if desired, with whipped cream and the reserved redcurrants.

*The fruit pulp can be used in tarts or combined with cream or custard in a redcurrant fool.

BRAMBLE (OR BLACKBERRY) FOOL

The berries for this recipe were picked in Scotland, where they are usually called "brambles". The pretty colour of this dessert exactly matched the purple and white heather with which I was able to decorate the table. (N.B. This recipe can be frozen in trays to make a really delicious ice cream — and the heather too can be frozen, for later use!)

Serves 8.

Ingredients		Imperial	Metric	American
Sugar syrup, made from sugar and				
water	Sugar	4 oz	125 gms	½ cup
	Water	¼ pint	150 ml	10 tbsps
Cleaned brambles		1 lb	450 gms	1 lb
Lightly whipped double cream		½ pint	275 ml	1¼ cups
2 egg whites				

Dissolve sugar in water in a medium sized saucepan, bring to the boil and continue boiling for 3 minutes. Put in the brambles and simmer gently until softened. Cool and purée in a liquidiser or by pressing through a sieve or mouli mill. (Reserve a few spoonfuls of purée). You may prefer to sieve after making a purée, in any case, to remove the seeds. Stir in the whipped cream, then lightly fold in the stiffly beaten egg whites. Spoon into glass dishes and top with a whirl of the reserved fruit purée.

Maureen Mooney

Cakes, Scones, Biscuits and Teabreads

Scotland is justly famous for its baking, its bakers and its bakeries. The latter go back in our culinary history a long, long way — in Edinburgh, we know, until at least the late 15th century. There is a very apparent "French influence" in our baking (epitomised in the sign I once saw above a Scottish baker's door — in Canada, incidentally — which read:—

"PATISSERIE PARISIENNE"
(Prop. A. McTavish)

In bakers' windows, éclairs, macaroons, custard slices (à la milles feuilles) and meringues share the glory with essentially Scottish teabreads (buns and loaves made from enriched, sweetened yeast dough) and local specialities such as Dundee cake, cream cookies, shortbread, scones, currant loaves and pancakes. The last named are thick, tender morsels, some 2½" (6 cm) across and not to be confused with either English pancakes or French "crèpes", which are much thinner and larger in circumference. I still use my grandmother's huge, iron griddle (often pronounced "Girdle") for baking pancakes and scones on top of the stove, as much Scottish baking used to be done and, for that matter, still is.

79

DUNDEE CAKE

Dundee is sometimes called the "city of the three J's" — the "J's" being Jute, Jam and Journalism — but "cake" might well be added to these three J's. It is my own theory that the following fruit cake may have acquired its name from a now famous Dundee bakery firm who might well have been the first to market this cake successfully — it is now tinned and exported all over the world.

Ingredients	Imperial	Metric	American
Softened margarine or butter	**8 oz**	**225 gms**	**1 cup**
Caster sugar	**8 oz**	**225 gms**	**1 cup**
5 eggs			
Plain flour	**8 oz**	**225 gms**	**2 cups**
Baking powder	**½ level tsp**	**½ x 5 ml spoon**	**½ tsp**
Pinch of salt			
Mixed dried fruit and peel	**12 oz**	**350 gms**	**2½ cups**
Blanched, split almonds or flaked almonds, to decorate	**2 oz**	**50 gms**	**⅓ cup**

Line a round cake tin, 8-9" (20-22 cm) in diameter, with kitchen foil or a double thickness of buttered, greaseproof paper. The lining should rise 1" (2½ cm) higher than the sides of the tin.

Cream margarine or butter and sugar. Beat in eggs, one at a time, adding 2 tbsps (2 x 15 ml spoons — 2 tbsps) sifted flour mixture after each egg. Stir in remaining flour, then the mixed fruit and peel. Turn into the lined tin and bake in a very moderate oven (325°F/170°C — mark 3) for 45 minutes before arranging the almonds over the surface of the cake. Return to the oven for approximately 1½ hours longer or until cake tests done, i.e. until it shrinks slightly from the sides of the tin and a skewer inserted in the centre comes out clean. Cool on a wire rack before stripping off the foil or paper lining.

SHORTBREAD

Shortbread must, I think, take pride of place amongst all Scottish baking and no Scottish household would be without it at "Hogmanay" (New Year's Eve). Traditionally, it is made in flat cakes, about ½" (1¼ cm) thick, sometimes formed in wooden shortbread moulds carved with thistles or other Scottish motifs, or it can be shaped into fingers, thin triangular "petticoat tails" or rounds. There is absolutely **no** substitute for butter in making shortbread.

Sift into a large bowl — 6 oz (175 gms — ¾ cup) plain flour, 1½ oz (40 gms — 5 tbsps) rice flour, a pinch each of baking powder and salt and 2 oz (50 gms — ¼ cup) caster sugar. Rub in 5 oz (150 gms — ½ cup + 2 tbsps) butter and knead to a firm, pliable dough. In the absence of a mould, it can be shaped into a large, ½" (1¼ cm) thick round about 6" (15 cm) in diameter, set on a baking sheet or sandwich tin, pricked with a fork at regular intervals and baked very slowly and patiently until straw coloured at 350°F/180°C — mark 4 for about 1 hour. Small thin biscuits may be ready in 12-15 minutes. Cool on a wire rack. Dredge with caster sugar when cold.

BLACK BUN

This could be described as an almost solid, spiced fruit mixture, enclosed in a glazed, almost pastry-like crust — but the description would not do it justice. Black bun is an expensive speciality these days, almost entirely reserved for Christmas and New Year festivities.

Ingredients	Imperial	Metric	American
For the pastry:			
Plain flour	1 lb	450 gms	4 cups
Baking powder	1 level tsp	1 x 5 ml spoon	1 tsp
Pinch of salt			
Butter	6 oz	175 gms	¾ cup
1 egg plus cold water to mix			
For the filling:			
Currants	2½ lbs	1¼ kg	7½ cups
Raisins (stoned Muscatels are best but not easily available)	1½ lbs	675 gms	4½ cups
Blanched almonds, chopped	8 oz	225 gms	1⅓ cups
Mixed peel, chopped	8 oz	225 gms	1⅓ cups
Plain flour	1 lb	450 gms	4 cups
Baking soda	½ level tsp	½ x 5 ml spoon	½ tsp
Cream of tartar	1 level tsp	1 x 5 ml spoon	1 tsp
Caster sugar	8 oz	225 gms	1 cup
Ground black pepper	½ level tsp	½ x 5 ml spoon	½ tsp
Ground allspice	½ level tsp	½ x 5 ml spoon	½ tsp
Ground ginger	1 level tsp	1 x 5 ml spoon	1 tsp
Ground cinnamon	1 level tsp	1 x 5 ml spoon	1 tsp

Milk and brandy to moisten

Sift flour, baking powder and salt into a large bowl for the pastry and rub in the butter. Stir in the beaten egg (reserving 1 tbsp (1 x 15 ml spoon — 1 tbsp) of it for glazing later) and enough cold water to bind to a firm dough. Roll out ⅔ of the pastry on a floured surface and use to line a greased, 8″ (20 cm) diameter cake tin. Roll out remaining pastry into a circle a little larger than the tin, and reserve as a "lid".

Mix fruit in a very large bowl, with nuts and peel. Mix together, then sift in the dry ingredients. Combine thoroughly. Add enough milk, roughly ¼ to ½ a pint (150 to 275 ml — 10 to 20 tbsps) and about 3 tbsps (3 x 15 ml spoons — 3 tsps) brandy to moisten. Turn fruit mixture into the lined tin. Brush the pastry lid with cold water and set, moistened side downwards, on top. Press edges together to seal well. Brush with reserved beaten egg, then prick top all over with a fork. Insert a skewer from the top through to the bottom of the bun at roughly 2″ (5 cm) intervals.

Bake in the centre of a very moderate oven (350°F/180°C — mark 4) until a skewer inserted in the centre comes out clean (about 3 hours). Black bun is best made 10-30 days in advance.

OATCAKES

An American guest once referred to these as "oatmeal tricorns" and I suppose this is a fair enough description. They are not the easiest of things to make well as the dough is inclined to be sticky. It is best to make a small quantity at a time, rubbing the board and the dough itself over with fine oatmeal, as necessary.

Start heating a griddle or heavy frying pan (dry) over gentle heat. Put 4 oz (125 gms — 1 cup) medium oatmeal into a mixing bowl and mix with a pinch of baking soda and a pinch of salt. Make a well in the centre. Pour into this ½ oz (15 gms — 1 tbsp) butter or fat, melted, and just enough hot water, roughly 3 tbsps (3 x 15 ml spoons — 3 tbsps) to bind into a firm dough. Rub a wooden board (the bread board will do in the absence of a baking board) with fine oatmeal and roll the dough out on this to a thickness of about ⅛″ (¼ cm). Cut into a neat round, using a 6″-7″ (15-18 cm) plate as a guide. Cut again into 4 or 8 triangles. Slip onto the hot griddle with a spatula, smooth side uppermost and cook until the edges begin to curl upwards, then remove to a rack. Finish cooking in a moderate oven (350°F/180°C — mark 4) until toasted crisp but not too brown.

Oatcakes are at their best when served freshly baked, with butter, marmalade, honey or cheese. They will, however, keep well in an air-tight tin.

CREAM COOKIES

American friends please note these are a type of cream filled bun and bear no resemblance to American "cookies", which we Scots call "biscuits". (Just to add to the confusion, Scots scones are very similar to American "biscuits"!)

Sift 1 lb (450 gms — 4 cup) of plain flour with 1 level tsp (1 x 5 ml — 1 tsp) salt and 2 oz (50 gms — ¼ cup) caster sugar into a mixing bowl. Melt 2 oz (50 gms — ¼ cup) butter in a teacupful (200 ml — ¾ cup) warm milk and stir in 1 beaten egg. In another small bowl, beat ¾ oz (20 gms — 3 dstps) baker's yeast to a cream with 1 tsp (1 x 5 ml spoon — 1 tsp) sugar, then stir in the milk mixture. Make a hollow in the flour and pour in the milk/yeast mixture. Gradually draw in the flour. Cover the basin with a tea towel which has been wrung out in hot water. Leave to rise to double volume. Cut into 12 pieces and roll each into a ball. Space out on a buttered baking sheet and leave to rise again in a warm place for about 30 minutes. Brush with melted butter before baking in a hot oven (425°F/220°C — mark 7) until well browned — about 20 minutes. Cool on a rack and, when cold, split almost all the way through and pipe in some stiffly whipped cream. Dust the tops of the cookies with sifted icing sugar.

SELKIRK BANNOCK

This is circular, very rich fruit loaf — flat on the bottom and rounded on top. It is usually served for tea, sliced and buttered. Few Scottish bakers fail to stock it.

Sift 1 lb (450 gms — 4 cups) strong plain flour with 1 level tsp (1 x 5 ml spoon — 1 tsp) salt into a mixing bowl. Rub in 2 oz (50 gms — ¼ cup) lard and 4 oz (125 gms — ½ cup) fresh butter. Stir in 4 oz (125 gms — ½ cup) caster sugar. In a small bowl, cream 1 oz (25 gms — 2 tbsps) baker's yeast with 2 level tsps (2 x 5 ml spoons — 2 tsps) sugar, then stir in a teacupful of warm milk. Pour this into a well in the centre of the dry mixture and gradually draw this in. Work in 1 lb (450 gms — 3 cups) of sultanas. Knead on a floured surface for 10 minutes, then place in a buttered 6-7" (15-18 cm) diameter cake tin, to rise. (In my modern method, I put the tin into an oiled polythene bag). When the bannock has nearly doubled in volume, bake it in a moderate oven (375°F/190°C — mark 5) until well browned. As soon as you take the bannock from the oven, brush it with a glaze made by melting a flat teaspoonful (1 x 5 ml spoon — 1 tsp) of sugar in 1 tbsp (1 x 15 ml spoon — 1 tbsp) warm milk. Cool on a wire rack.

GRANNY'S CAKE

This was a favourite, quick "stand-by" of my grandmother's when we had unexpected company for tea. She made it in a 1½" (4 cm) deep, oblong baking tin (which I still use and identify as "Granny's Cake Tin") and cut the cake into squares while in the tin. We liked it best served still slightly warm.

Ingredients	Imperial	Metric	American
Plain flour	8 oz	225 gms	2 cups
Pinch of salt			
Baking powder	2 tsps	2 x 5 ml spoons	2 tsps
Butter or margarine	2 oz	50 gms	¼ cup
Caster sugar	4 oz	125 gms	½ cup
2 eggs			
Milk	¼ pint	150 ml	10 tbsps
Vanilla essence	¼ tsp	¼ x 5 ml spoon	¼ tsp
Water icing:			
Icing sugar	4 oz	125 gms	1 cup
A little hot water			
Few drops vanilla essence			

Prepare a 9" x 12" (22 x 30 cm) baking tin or a square cake tin, at least 1½" (4 cm) deep, by rubbing the inside over with butter paper and dredging it with flour. Sieve flour, salt and baking powder into a mixing bowl, rub in the butter with the fingertips until the mixture resembles fine breadcrumbs, then mix in the sugar. Break the eggs into a small bowl, place this bowl in a larger bowl or a pan containing hot water, then switch the eggs with a rotary beater until very light. Stir the eggs into the flour mixture, gradually add the milk and beat well. Pour the mixture into the prepared cake tin and bake in a pre-heated, moderate oven (375°F/190°C — mark 5) for 25-30 minutes or until cake tests done (i.e. a wooden cocktail stick or thin skewer should come out clean when inserted in the middle of the cake).

Mix the icing sugar with just enough hot water to bring it to a spreading consistency and add a few drops of vanilla essence. Spread icing over the cake while it is still warm and serve.

PANCAKES (or "DROP SCONES")

These pancakes should be about ⅜" (1 cm) thick and 3 inches (7½ cm) across and are usually made on a Scotch "girdle" but a thick-based frying pan or the solid plate on an electric stove (at medium heat) can be used with equal success. Have them for tea with butter, syrup or jam.

Ingredients	Imperial	Metric	American
Plain flour	6 oz	175 gms	¾ cup
Baking soda	½ tsp	½ x 5 ml spoon	½ tsp
Cream of tartar	1 tsp	1 x 5 ml spoon	1 tsp
Pinch of salt			
Sugar	2 oz	50 gms	¼ cup
1 egg			
½ teacup milk	Approx 4 fl oz	125 ml	½ cup

Sift all dry ingredients into a mixing bowl; switch the egg and milk together in another bowl; make a well in the flour mixture and gradually stir in the egg and milk, to form a thick, pouring batter. Beat very thoroughly. (The batter is all the better if allowed to stand for about an hour but this is not essential).

Heat the girdle or pan and grease with a little fat on a piece of butter paper — it is hot enough to use when a drop of water sizzles and evaporates immediately on its surface. Drop batter onto the hot girdle in large spoonfuls (or pour it carefully from a jug) keeping the pancakes well apart. When bubbles appear on the top, the pancakes are ready for turning — they should be golden brown on each side. Wrap the pancakes in a napkin or tea-towel as they are cooked.

TREACLE PANCAKES

Makes about 1½ dozen.

Ingredients	Imperial	Metric	American
Plain flour	6 oz	175 gms	¾ cup
Baking soda	½ level tsp	½ x 5 ml spoon	½ tsp
Cream of tartar	1 level tsp	1 x 5 ml spoon	1 tsp
Pinch of salt			
Caster sugar	1 oz	25 gms	2 tbsps
Milk, warmed to blood heat	4 fl oz	125 ml	½ cup
Dark treacle	1 tbsp	1 x 15 ml spoon	1 tbsp
1 egg, beaten			

Sift flour, baking soda, cream of tartar and salt into a mixing bowl. Stir in caster sugar. Warm the milk slightly and stir into it the treacle and beaten egg. Make a well in the flour mixture and gradually stir in the liquid, to form a thick, pouring batter. Beat thoroughly until smooth.

Heat the griddle or pan and grease with a little fat on a piece of butter paper — it is hot enough to use when a drop of water sizzles and evaporates immediately on its surface. Drop batter in tablespoonful onto the griddle, allowing space for it to spread. When bubbles appear on the top, the pancakes are ready for turning. Re-grease the griddle before cooking the next batch.

Serve with butter and treacle or golden syrup.

POTATO SCONES

Makes 1 dozen.

Ingredients	Imperial	Metric	American
Warm mashed potatoes	½ lb	225 gms	½ lb
Plain or self-raising flour	4 oz	125 gms	1 cup
Pinch of salt			

Mix all ingredients together to a firm, smooth dough. Divide into two portions and roll each out on a floured surface to not more than ⅛″ (½ cm) thick. Using a 7″ (18-19 cm) teaplate as a guide, cut two rounds and divide each round into four triangles. Gather up the scraps and roll out into a third circle, then cut into four.

Cook on top of the stove on a lightly greased griddle, solid hot plate or heavy frying pan, browning quickly on each side. The scones will have a speckled appearance. Cook a few at a time, greasing the griddle again with butter paper before making the next batch.

Potato scones are delicious either hot or cold, spread with butter, and/or cheese — or try them fried for breakfast, with grilled bacon and tomato.

GRAN GOW'S GRIDDLE SCONES

Cook some of these tender little "top of the stove" scones to spread with newly made jam or to store in the freezer.

Makes about 12.

Ingredients	Imperial	Metric	American
8 heaped tbsps self-raising flour	About 8 oz	225 gms	2 cups
Baking powder	2 level tsps	2 x 5 ml spoons	2 tsps
Cream of tartar	1 level tsp	1 x 5 ml spoon	1 tsp
Caster sugar	2 level tsps	2 x 5 ml spoons	2 tsps
2 eggs			
Milk	¼ pint	150 ml	10 tbsps
Walnut sized piece of butter, melted			

Start heating a griddle or large frying pan over just less than medium heat. Sift dry ingredients into a large bowl. Break in the whole eggs and stir, then stir in milk and lastly the melted butter. The batter should be of a soft, dropping consistency.

Dip heaped dessertspoons of batter into a little flour, to coat them, turning them in the flour with your hands, then patting each scone out into rounds about ½" (1¼ cm) thick. Put onto the heated, very lightly greased griddle or pan and cook until speckled deep brown on each side — the scones will require longer on the first side than the second.

Wrap, as cooked, in a napkin, laid on a wire tray. (These are the best griddle scones I know — and just as good with butter and cheese as with jam).

To Freeze: When cold, seal in polythene bags and freeze.

To re-heat: Allow to thaw at room temperature and warm slightly in the oven.

FATTY CUTTIES

A recipe from Westray in the Outer North Isles of Orkney. The crunchy, between-shortbread-and-scone texture is most unusual and very, very good. Enjoy them with tea or coffee.

Makes 32 (**not** too many — they disappear like magic from the tin).

Ingredients	Imperial	Metric	American
3 level teacups plain flour			
Baking soda	⅛th level tsp	⅛ x 5 ml spoon	⅛ tsp
1 level teacup sugar — caster or granulated			
1 level teacup currants*			
Margarine or butter, melted	8 oz	225 gms	1 cup

Sift flour and soda together into a large bowl. Mix in sugar and currants. Stir in melted fat, to make a stiff dough. Knead smooth on a floured surface. Divide into four and roll out each piece as thinly as possible — about ⅛″ (½ cm) thick. Cut each circle into 8 wedges and bake 4 wedges at a time (you need to flip them over) on a **slow, ungreased** girdle or frying pan, over moderate heat, until golden brown, turning only once. They will probably take about 10 minutes on the first side and 8 to 10 minutes on the second. Cool on a wire rack — they will become crisp as they cool.

Note — The dough is very crumbly and you will have to handle and turn it with care.

*I substituted mixed dried fruit with peel, when I was short of currants, and liked the resulting fatty cutties even better.

BERE BANNOCKS

If you want to make authentic bere bannocks, the bere meal is obtainable from Stronsay Meal Mill, Stronsay, Orkney — or you can substitute fine-ground wholemeal flour for it. There is an old superstition that it is good luck to stir bannocks clockwise — and bere meal is said to sweeten both the temper and the complexion!

Makes 1 large bannock — 8 good sized wedges.

Ingredients	Imperial	Metric	American
Bere meal	4 oz	125 gms	¾ cup
Plain flour	4 oz	125 gms	1 cup
Baking soda	1 level tsp	1 x 5 ml spoon	1 tsp
Cream of tartar	½ level tsp	½ x 5 ml spoon	½ tsp
Salt	¼ level tsp	¼ x 5 ml spoon	¼ tsp

1 egg

Mix bere meal and flour with baking soda, cream of tartar and salt in a large bowl. Switch egg lightly with a cupful of the milk and draw into the flour. Stir in more milk as necessary to make a soft dough. Turn onto a floured board and pat out about ½″ (1¼ cm) thick, into a circle. Neaten the edges by pressing inwards with the flat of a knife.

Bake, over moderate heat, on a lightly greased "girdle" or frying pan until browned on each side, turning only once — up to 10 minutes on the first side and 5 on the second.

Eat hot or cold, spread with butter — good too with cheese.

OVEN SCONES

Makes 1 dozen.

Ingredients	Imperial	Metric	American
Self-raising flour*	8 oz	225 gms	2 cups
Baking powder	1 level tsp	1 x 5 ml spoon	1 tsp
Pinch of salt			
Margarine	2 oz	50 gms	¼ cup
Caster sugar	1 oz	25 gms	2 tbsps
Milk to mix	About 5 tbsps	5 x 15 ml spoons	5 tbsps

A little milk or beaten egg, to brush
 tops

Sift flour, baking powder and salt into a large mixing bowl.

Rub in margarine, then stir in sugar. Using a fork, stir in enough milk to make a soft dough. Turn onto a floured surface and pat out gently until ¾"-1" (2-2½ cm) thick. Use a small cutter (plain or fluted) to cut rounds and place on slightly greased baking sheet. Brush tops with a little milk or beaten egg.

Bake just above centre in a moderately hot oven (400°F/200°C — mark 6) until well risen and lightly browned. Serve fresh from the oven, if possible, with butter and jam.

*or plain flour + 1 x 5 ml spoon (1 tsp) extra baking powder.

Preserves

Many a remote Highland farmhouse now boasts a handsome, big deep freeze but this will never altogether replace the well stocked preserves cupboard which is the Scottish housewife's pride. The sight of jams, chutneys and pickles, in shining, labelled rows, creates a glow of satisfaction which no other type of culinary art quite achieves, perhaps because of its comparitively lasting evidence of industry and of thoughtful providence in storing away some of summer's goodness for a literally rainy day.

The summer soft fruit harvest comes considerably later in Scotland than in more southerly climates but, in spite — or perhaps because — of this, it ripens slowly to a sweet perfection unmatched anywhere. From July onwards, strawberries, raspberries, gooseberries, red and blackcurrants crop in abundance and, in the autumn, there are brambles, rowans, elderberries and plenty of small but juicy apples to top up the preserves cupboard with jams, jellies and wine.

But it is in the depths of winter that Scotland's most renowned preserve — marmalade — is concocted from bitter oranges, imported from Seville. For we can truly claim that marmalade was invented in Scotland, at the beginning of the 18th century, by one James Keiller a merchant of Dundee (or perhaps his wife?), who could not resist a shipment of cheap but bitter oranges, which proved otherwise unsaleable.

SEVILLE ORANGE MARMALADE

This marmalade sets very quickly to a firm jelly and has an excellent flavour, as well as being extremely economical.

Makes 10 to 11 lbs (4½ to 5 kg) from 2 lbs (1 kg) Seville oranges.

Wash the 2 lbs (1 kg — 2 lbs) of Seville oranges. Cut fruit across and squeeze out the juice, carefully removing the pips and placing them in a separate small basin.

For thick, chunky marmalade — put fruit through a mincing machine, using the large hole plate; if preferred, shred skins into thin slices using a sharp knife. Put fruit into a large basin with the juice and 6 pints (3¼ litres — 15 cups) cold water. Pips should be tied in muslin in the small basin and 1 pint (575 ml — 2½ cups) boiling water poured over. Cover both basins and leave to stand for 24 hours.

Next day, strain liquid and jelly from the pips into a preserving pan along with the fruit juice and pulp. Add bag of pips. Cook gently until peel is tender — 1½ to 2 hours. Remove pan from heat and let stand another 24 hours.

3rd Day. To each measured pint (575 ml — 2½ cups) of pulp, add 1 lb (450 gms — 2 cups) sugar — preserving sugar for preference but ordinary granulated sugar will do. Heat gently until all sugar has dissolved, then raise heat to fast boil and cook quickly until ready to set. Test by dropping a small amount of marmalade onto a saucer — as it cools, it should wrinkle when pushed gently across the surface with a finger. Remove from heat, stand for 5 minutes then stir briefly before pouring into clean, hot jars. Cover and seal at once.

APPLE, MARROW AND GINGER MARMALADE

Yields about 5 lbs (2¼ kg — 5 lbs).

Ingredients	Imperial	Metric	American
Vegetable marrow (weighed when peeled and cored)	2 lbs	1 kg	2 lbs
Preserving or crystallised ginger	¼ lb	125 gms	4 oz
Sugar	2 lbs	1 kg	4 cups
Apple juice (obtained from tart apples, just covered with Apples:	3 pints / 4 lbs	1¾ litres / 1¾ kg	7½ cups / 4 lbs
water, simmered until Water: soft, then strained)	1½ pints	850 ml	3¾ cups
Strained juice of 1 lemon			

Peel, scoop out centre pulp and chop marrow into very fine dice. Slice ginger as thinly as possible then chop into small pieces. Layer marrow and ginger with sugar and leave covered overnight.

Quarter but do not peel or core apples, removing only the blemishes. Just cover with water and simmer gently until thoroughly soft and pulpy. Strain through a scalded jelly bag.

Next day, measure juice into a large preserving pan. Add all the other ingredients. Bring very slowly to the boil and simmer (do not fast boil) over medium heat until marrow is clear and a set is obtained — roughly ½ hour. The safest test for a set is one of the oldest — pour a little hot jam or jelly onto a saucer and, when cool, it should wrinkle when gently pushed across the surface with a finger.

Pot and seal at once in hot, sterile jars.

This is a very good breakfast or tea-time preserve.

DRIED APPLE RINGS

These can be very useful in compotes (e.g. with apricots and figs) and I particularly value them for adding to home-made breakfast meusli.

Peel and core the apples and cut them into rings about ¼" (¾ cm) thick. Make a salt solution using 1½ oz (3 x 15 ml spoons — 3 tbsps) salt to a gallon of water and dip apple rings into this for 3-4 minutes. Drain and thread the rings onto sticks or skewers, balancing them over a baking tin. Place in a cool oven (200°F/100°C — mark ¼) until rings are dry and leathery — about 6 to 8 hours. Store in bottles in a cool dry place, once absolutely cold.

STRAWBERRY JAM

Even if you seldom use jam, a small horde of home-made strawberry jam will come in useful — and the taste of newly made strawberry jam is a once-a-year treat not to be missed. Try it on buttered scones or pancakes with whipped cream.

Yields about 5 lbs (2¼ kg).

Ingredients	Imperial	Metric	American
Just ripe strawberries, weighed after cleaning	**3½ lbs**	**1½ kg**	**3½ lbs**
Strained lemon juice	**5 tbsps**	**5 x 15 ml spoons**	**5 tbsps**
Preserving sugar (or granulated)	**3 lbs**	**1¼ kg**	**6 cups**

Wash and hull the strawberries and remove any small blemishes. Cut any extra large berries in half. Put berries and lemon juice in a large pan and heat very gently until the juice runs and the berries are soft. Add the sugar and stir with a wooden spoon, over medium heat, until sugar has dissolved. Bring slowly to the boil, then boil very rapidly for 15-20 minutes or until a set is obtained. (Start testing for a set after 15 minutes by cooling a little jam on a saucer — the surface should wrinkle when pushed gently with a finger).

Remove from heat and take off any scum, using a metal spoon. Ladle into hot, sterile jars and seal immediately. (To sterilise jars, wash in hot, soapy water, rinse thoroughly and dry off upside down in the oven).

RASPBERRY JAM

Yields about 6 lbs (2¾ kg — 6 lbs).

Wash and clean 4 lbs (1¾ kg — 4 lbs) raspberries. If fruit is just ripe, add 5 tbsps (5 x 15 ml spoons) cold water. Heat very gently in a large pan until tender. Add 3½ lbs (1¼ kg — 7 cups) sugar (preserving or granulated), stir until dissolved and bring slowly to the boil. Raise heat and boil rapidly until a set is obtained — start testing after 15 minutes. Usual setting time is 15-20 minutes but this will vary. Pot in hot, sterile jars and seal immediately.

BRAMBLE JAM

Absolutely lovely with hot scones or toast!

Yeilds about 4½ lbs (2 kg — 4½ lbs).

Ingredients	Imperial	Metric	American
Brambles	2½ lbs	1½ kg	2½ lbs
Sugar	2 lbs	1 kg	4 cups

Heat the washed brambles (having removed any husks) gently without water until juicy and soft. Add sugar and stir over low heat until dissolved. Boil quickly until set — about 20 minutes. Skim, pot and cover at once.

APRICOT JAM

Ingredients	Imperial	Metric	American
Dried apricots	1 lb	450 gms	1 lb
Water	3 pints	1¾ litres	7½ cups
1 lemon			
Sugar	2½ lbs	1¼ kg	5 cups

Wash the fruit and chop roughly. Cover with the measured cold water and leave to soak overnight. Next day, add lemon juice and bring to the boil. Simmer gently for about 30 minutes, stirring occasionally. Add sugar and stir over low heat until dissolved. Bring to a fast boil, stirring frequently, and continue until a set is obtained. If you are using a sugar thermometer, the temperature should read 219-220°F (104°C) and a little of the jam, cooled quickly in a saucer, should form a thin skin which wrinkles across the surface when you push it gently with your fingers. Pot in warm, sterile jars. Cover and seal either immediately or when absolutely cold.

PLUM OR GREENGAGE JAM

Yields about 7 lbs (3 kg — 7 lbs).

Ingredients	Imperial	Metric	American
Plums	**3 lbs**	**1½ kg**	**3 lbs**
Water	**1 pint**	**575 ml**	**2½ cups**
Sugar	**3 lbs**	**1½ kg**	**6 cups**

Wash, halve and stone the fruit, removing blemishes. Simmer with the water and sugar until sugar has dissolved, then boil rapidly. It will be ready to set in 15-20 minutes. Pot and seal, as usual.

GREEN GOOSEBERRY JAM

Makes about 10 lbs (4½ kg).

Ingredients	Imperial	Metric	American
Unripe green gooseberries	**3 lbs**	**1¼ kg**	**3 lbs**
Water	**2½ pints**	**1.625 l**	**6¼ cups**
Sugar	**5 lbs**	**2¼ kg**	**10 cups**

Top, tail and wash berries. In a large pan, boil very gently in the water for 1 hour. Add sugar and stir over low heat until it has dissolved, then bring to a fast boil. A rapid set is usually obtained with this jam, so start testing after 3 minutes. Pot and seal in the usual way.

APPLE JELLY

Ingredients	Imperial	Metric	American
Windfall apples, or any tart apples (weigh after cutting off any blemishes)	**6 lbs**	**2¾ kg**	**6 lbs**
8 cloves			
Water	**3 pints**	**1¾ litres**	**7½ cups**
Sugar	**2½-3 lbs**	**1¼ kg**	**5-6 cups**
Juice of 1 lemon			

Wash and quarter the apples but do not peel or core; put apples, cloves and water in a large pan, bring quickly to the boil, then simmer gently until apples are pulped (about 1½ hours); strain through a jelly-bag overnight.

Measure the juice into a large pan and for each pint (575 ml — 2½ cups) of juice add 1 lb (450 gms —2 cups) of sugar. Add the lemon juice, bring slowly to the boil, then boil rapidly and start testing for a set after about 10 minutes. When a little juice, poured into a saucer and allowed to cool, forms a thin skin and wrinkles when you draw your finger lightly across it, the jelly will set. Remove any scum. Pot and cover while hot.

The jars should be washed, dried in the oven and used while still hot.

MINT JELLY

This can be made with tart, green apples, in the same way as the apple jelly, substituting a large bunch of fresh mint for the cloves and adding ½ tsp (½ x 5 ml spoon — ½ tsp) citric acid to each 2 lb (1 kg — 2 lb) of apples. A few drops of green colouring improves the appearance.

*TART JELLY

Yields about 7 lbs (3 kg).

Ingredients	Imperial	Metric	American
Redcurrants	2 lbs	1 kg	2 lbs
Gooseberries (barely ripe)	1 lb	450 gms	1 lb
Rhubarb	1 lb	450 gms	1 lb
Citric acid	1 level tsp	1 x 5 ml spoon	1 tsp

Wash the fruit and chop the rhubarb into ½"-1" (1¼-2½ cm) lengths. (The redcurrants and gooseberries do not have to be topped or tailed). Put the fruit into a large pan, just cover with water and bring slowly to the boil. Simmer gently until fruit is pulpy and soft. Turn into a jelly bag suspended over a large basin and allow juice to drip through overnight.

Measure the juice and for each pint (575 ml — 2½ cups) add 1 lb (450 gms — 2 cups) sugar, in a large pan. Stir over gentle heat until sugar has dissolved. Add citric acid, bring to the boil and boil rapidly until a set is obtained — roughly 15 to 20 minutes. To test for a set, cool a little of the potential jelly as quickly as possible on a saucer — when the jelly wrinkles as you push a finger gently across the surface, it is ready to set.

Pot and seal at once (or when completely cold) in hot, sterile jars. Small jars are best, so that one complete jar can be used to glaze a tart or serve as an accompaniment to meat. Store in a cool, dry place.

To use as a glaze, simply melt the jelly in a small pan and spoon it, while still warm, over the fruit. It will quickly set again.

*This preserve is "tart" in two senses — it has a fine, tangy flavour and is very good for glazing fruit tarts, as well as being much less costly than pure redcurrant jelly.

ELDERBERRY JELLY

Pick the berries when they are black and plump. Wash the berries and remove them from the stalks — it is quickest to do this with a fork. Measure 2 pints (1 litre — 5 cups) of berries and 1 pint (½ litre — 2½ cups) cold water into a pan and simmer until soft.

Meanwhile, wash and quarter (but do not peel or core) 2 lbs (1 kg — 2 lbs) of small, tart apples (crab apples or windfalls are good), add 1 pint (½ litre —

2½ cups) water and simmer until soft.

The two fruits are simmered separately as one may require longer than the other to soften and flavour is always impaired by over-cooking.

Turn both lots of fruit into a jelly bag suspended over a large bowl and allow the juice to finish dripping through. Measure the juice into a large pan. Bring to the boil, then add 1 lb (450 gms — 2 cups) sugar to each pint (575 ml — 2½ cups) of juice. Stir until sugar has dissolved, then boil fairly rapidly until a set is obtained — it will probably set quite quickly, perhaps in as little as 10 minutes. (To test for a set, drip a little of the liquid into a saucer and cool it quickly — if it wrinkles when you push a forefinger gently across the surface, it is ready to set). Remove from heat and skim, if necessary, any pale frothy substance from the surface.

Pour into hot, sterile jars and seal immediately.

REDCURRANT JELLY

Ingredients	Imperial	Metric	American
Redcurrants	4 lbs	1¾ kg	4 lbs
Water	1 pint	575 ml	2½ cups
Sugar for each pint of juice obtained	1 lb	450 gms	2 cups

Wash the fruit but it is not necessary to remove the stalks; put the fruit and water into a large pan and simmer gently until the fruit is reduced to a pulp. Empty the pulp into a jelly bag and allow all the juice to drip through — this can be done overnight. Measure the juice into a large pan and add 1 lb (450 gms — 2½ cups) of sugar for each pint (575 ml — 2½ cups) of juice. Boil rapidly and start testing for a set after ten minutes. When a little juice, poured into a saucer and allowed to cool, forms a thin skin and wrinkles when you draw your finger lightly across it, the jelly will set. Remove any scum with a spoon. Pot and cover while hot. (The jars should be washed, dried in the oven and used while hot).

BLACKCURRANT JAM

(This is one of the easiest jams to make).

Ingredients	Imperial	Metric	American
Blackcurrants	4 lbs	1¾ kg	4 lbs
Water	4 pints	2.300 l	10 cups
Sugar	8 lbs	3½ kg	16 cups

Clean the fruit, put in a large pan with the water, bring to the boil and simmer until the fruit is tender (10-20 minutes); add the sugar, bring slowly to the boil and start testing for a set after ten minutes. Pour into hot, sterilised jars and cover while hot.

GOOSEBERRY CHUTNEY

(An especially good chutney with cold meats).

Ingredients	Imperial	Metric	American
Gooseberries (red or green)	4 lbs	1¾ kg	4 lbs
Onions chopped	½ lb	225 gms	½ lb
Vinegar	1 pint	575 ml	2½ cups
Ground ginger	1 tsp	1 x 5 ml spoon	1 tsp
Sugar	1 lb	450 gms	2 cups
Cinnamon	½ tsp	½ x 5 ml spoon	½ tsp
Nutmeg	¼ tsp	¼ x 5 ml spoon	¼ tsp
Cloves	¼ tsp	¼ x 5 ml spoon	¼ tsp
Tabasco	¼ tsp	¼ x 5 ml spoon	¼ tsp

Put all ingredients except the berries into a large pan and boil for 10 minutes. Add gooseberries and boil for a further 20 minutes, or until thick. Put into hot, sterile jars and seal.

RHUBARB CHUTNEY

Makes about 7½ lbs (3¼ kg).

Ingredients	Imperial	Metric	American
Rhubarb, finely chopped	3 lbs	1¼ kg	3 lbs
Apples, peeled, cored and chopped	1 lb	450 gms	1 lb
Onions, finely chopped	½ lb	225 gms	½ lb
Sultanas	1 lb	450 gms	3 cups
Vinegar	1 pint	575 ml	2½ cups
Sugar	1 lb	450 gms	2 cups
Salt	1 level tsp	1 x 5 ml spoon	1 tsp
Ginger	1 level tsp	1 x 5 ml spoon	1 tsp
Curry powder (optional)	2 level tsps	2 x 5 ml spoons	2 tsps

Put all ingredients into a large pan, bring slowly to the boil and cook gently for about 1 hour or until soft, stirring occasionally. Pack into hot, sterile jars and seal at once or when completely cold.

LEMON CURD

A treat for the tea table and a delicious preserve for filling tarts, sponges or meringues.

Yields about 2½ lbs (1-1¼ kg — 2½ lbs).

Ingredients	Imperial	Metric	American
4 large lemons			
5 standard eggs, lightly beaten			
Fresh butter	**4 oz**	**125 gms**	**½ cup**
Sugar	**1 lb**	**450 gms**	**2 cups**

Wash and dry lemons. Grate off all rind finely. Squeeze out juice and put juice and rind in a thick saucepan. Add eggs, butter and sugar and cook over very low heat, stirring continuously with a wooden spoon, until mixture thickens. Pot in hot, sterile jars and seal at once.

REDCURRANT AND GOOSEBERRY JELLY

Redcurrants are often in shorter supply than other soft fruits and usually very expensive — mixed with gooseberries they make an excellent and economical preserve, either for the tea table or as a glaze, and tart enough too to use with lamb or game dishes.

Yields approximately 3 lbs (1¼ kg — 3 lbs).

Ingredients	Imperial	Metric	American
Unripe gooseberries (either red or green)	**2 lbs**	**1 kg**	**2 lbs**
Redcurrants	**1 lb**	**450 gms**	**1 lb**
Water	**1 pint**	**275 ml**	**2½ cups**
Sugar to each pint juice obtained	**1 lb**	**450 gms**	**2 cups**

Wash the fruit but it is not necessary to top and tail or to remove stalks. Place fruit in a pan with the water and simmer gently until pulpy. Empty into a scalded jelly bag, suspended over a large bowl, and allow juice to drip through.

Measure juice into a large pan and add 1 lb (450 gms — 2 cups) sugar to each pint (575 ml — 2½ cups) of juice. Stir over low heat until sugar dissolves, then boil rapidly and start testing for a set after 10 minutes — see "strawberry jam" recipe for testing set. Using a sugar thermometer, the reading should be 220°F/120°C. When ready, remove from heat and take away any scum, using a metal spoon. Pot in hot, sterile jars (small jars are handy, so that one may be enough each time used) and seal immediately.

APPLE CHUTNEY

Ingredients	Imperial	Metric	American
Cooking apples, peeled, cored and chopped	1½ lbs	675 gms	1½ lbs
Sultanas	½ lb	225 gms	1½ cups
Onions, peeled and chopped	½ lb	225 gms	½ lb
Brown sugar	6 oz	175 gms	¾ cup
Cooking salt	1 oz	25 gms	2 tbsps
Ground ginger	2 level tsps	2 x 5 ml spoons	2 tsps
Ground cloves	¼ level tsp	¼ x 5 ml spoon	¼ tsp
Curry powder (optional)	½ level tsp	½ x 5 ml spoon	½ tsp
Tabasco	¼ tsp	¼ x 5 ml spoon	¼ tsp
Vinegar	1 pint	275 ml	1¼ cups

Bring all ingredients slowly to the boil in a saucepan (do not use a copper or brass pan for chutneys which include vinegar). Simmer gently until soft. Pour into hot, dry jars and cover either while very hot or when quite cold.

SPICED VINEGAR

For pickles and sauces this keeps well in a screw top bottle or jar and is useful to have on hand in the preserving season.

Ingredients	Imperial	Metric	American
Vinegar	2 pints	1.150 litres	5 cups
2 blades mace			
8 peppercorns			
1 stick cinnamon			
8 cloves			
12 allspice berries			

Heat all ingredients slowly together in a saucepan, to boiling point.

Cover and let stand until cold. Strain and use or bottle. (If preferred, 4 heaped tbsps (4 heaped 15 ml spoons — 4 heaped tbsps) "pickling spices" which can be bought packaged as such, can be used in place of the above spices.)

CRANBERRY RELISH

Ingredients	Imperial	Metric	American
Fresh or frozen cranberries	8 oz	225 gms	8 oz
Sugar	6 oz	175 gms	¾ cup
Juice of 1 orange, made up to ¼ pint with water	¼ pint	150 ml	5 fl oz
Finely chopped rind of 1 orange			

Stew gently together until berries are tender but not too mushy — about 10 minutes. Serve cold. Traditional with "Bubbly Jock" — i.e. turkey.

ROWAN JELLY

This is an excellent accompaniment to strong-flavoured meat — anything from a haunch of venison to a rabbit pie.

Use an equal quantity of rowan berries — which should be just or not quite ripe, i.e. orange rather than red and very plump and firm — and tart apples. Remove rowan berries from their stalks, wash and drain. Quarter and remove blemishes (do not peel or core) from the apples. Just cover fruit with cold water and simmer until soft. Strain through a jelly bag.

Add 1 lb (450 gms — 2 cups) sugar to each pint (575 ml — 2½ cups) of juice measured into a large jelly pan. Optionally, one or two cloves and a strip of thinly pared lemon rind to each pint of juice can be tied in muslin and added to the pan. Boil rapidly until a set is obtained — roughly half an hour. Skim, pour into small, hot jars and seal at once.

PICKLED BEETROOT

This is a favourite pickle in Scotland, usually served with cold meat, but I like it too with potato-topped meat or fish pies and even with macaroni and cheese.

1 pint (575 ml — 2½ cups) spiced vinegar is sufficient to pickle 2 lbs (1 kg — 2 lbs) of beetroot. Wash the beetroot but do not cut off all the roots or tops — if you cut into the flesh, the beetroot will "bleed" and lose some of its rich colour when boiling.

Cover in mild brine using 1 oz (25 gms — 2 tbsps) salt to 4 pints water, in a large saucepan. Bring to the boil and simmer until tender — 1½ to 2 hours. Allow to cool in the liquid in the pan. When cold, the skins will slip off very easily — but do use rubber gloves to avoid staining your hands. Slice the beetroot fairly thin and pack closely in sterile screw-top jars. Cover with cold spiced vinegar and screw down.

HOT BANANA CHUTNEY

The ingredients for this have the advantage of being available all year round and the chutney has an intriguing "tropical but not too hot" flavour which I think you will like.

Yields about 5 lbs (2¼ kg — 5 lbs).

Ingredients	*Imperial*	*Metric*	*American*
Onions, finely chopped	**1 lb**	**450 gms**	**1 lb**
6 good sized bananas, finely chopped			
Cooking apples (weighed after peeling and coring) finely chopped	**½ lb**	**225 gms**	**½ lb**
Stoned, chopped cooking dates	**8 oz**	**225 gms**	**1 cup**
Sultanas	**4 oz**	**125 gms**	**¾ cup**
Salt	**2 level tbsps**	**2 x 15 ml spoons**	**2 tbsps**
Curry powder	**1 level tbsp**	**1 x 15 ml spoon**	**1 tbsp**
Ground allspice (freshly ground from the whole berries if possible — I use a pepper mill for this)	**1 level tsp**	**1 x 5 ml spoon**	**1 tsp**
Ground ginger	**1 level tsp**	**1 x 5 ml spoon**	**1 tsp**
Demerara or soft brown sugar	**½ lb**	**225 gms**	**1⅛ cups**
Brown malt vinegar	**1 pint**	**575 ml**	**2½ cups**

Combine all ingredients in a large pan (not copper or brass). Bring to the boil and simmer gently, stirring now and then, until soft, thick and pulpy — roughly an hour. Pot in hot, sterile jars and seal immediately.

PICKLED ONIONS

The best results are obtained from the simplest method I know — buy small, pickling onions and, if you suffer easily from streaming eyes, try peeling them below water (the onions, not you!) Place an upturned dinner plate on a tray and arrange onions on the plate, then sprinkle them with salt and leave overnight. The salt will liquify and the drips are caught in the tray. Rinse onions, pack in clean jars which have been dried in the oven. Add a few allspice berries and dried red chillies (both optional) to each jar, fill up with ordinary brown malt vinegar and seal. If you can resist the temptation to eat them for at least a month, so much the better.

GREEN TOMATO CHUTNEY

Yields about 12 lbs (5½ kg — 12 lbs).

Ingredients	Imperial	Metric	American
Chopped green tomatoes	7 lbs	3¼ kg	7 lbs
Chopped onions	1½ lbs	¾ kg	1 lb
Chopped apples (weighed after peeling and coring)	1½ lbs	¾ kg	1½ lbs
Demerara sugar	2 lbs	1 kg	4½ cups
Vinegar	½ pint	275 ml	1¼ cups
Curry powder	1 level tsp	1 x 5 ml spoon	1 tsp
Dried tamarind, chopped (Delicatessen shops specialising in herbs and spices will have this)	2 oz	50 gms	2 oz
Salt	2 oz	50 gms	2 tbsps
Allspice berries and peppercorns, ground in a pepper mill Each	1 dstsp	2 x 5 ml	1 dstsp
Ground cloves	1 level tsp	1 x 5 ml spoon	1 tsp
Black treacle	2 tbsps	2 x 15 ml spoons	2 tbsps

Put all ingredients into a large pan (not copper or brass). Bring slowly to the boil and simmer until pulpy — about 2½ hours. Bottle in hot, sterile jars and seal at once.

MARROW CHUTNEY

Yields about 8 lbs (3½ kg — 8 lbs).

Ingredients	Imperial	Metric	American
Vegetable marrow, peeled and diced (seedy centre section removed)	3 lbs	1¼ kg	3 lbs
Salt	2 level tsps	2 x 5 ml spoons	2 tsps
Onions or shallots, chopped	½ lb	225 gms	½ lb
Tart apples, peeled, cored and chopped	½ lb	225 gms	½ lb
Sultanas	½ lb	225 gms	1½ cups
Allspice berries and peppercorns, ground in a pepper mill Each	1 dstsp	2 x 5 ml spoons	1 dstsp
Ground ginger	1 level tsp	1 x 5 ml spoon	1 tsp
Ground cinnamon	¼ level tsp	¼ x 5 ml spoon	¼ tsp

101

Ingredients	Imperial	Metric	American
Soft brown sugar	**4 oz**	**125 gms**	**½ cup**
Malt vinegar	**1 pint**	**575 ml**	**2½ cups**

Layer the marrow with sprinkled salt and let stand overnight. Rinse marrow next day in cold water and drain thoroughly in a colander. Put marrow and all remaining ingredients into a large saucepan (not brass or copper) and bring slowly to the boil. Simmer gently until pulpy. Pot in hot, sterile jars and seal immediately.

This is a very good chutney to serve with hot or cold meats of any kind, or with cheese or savouries.

BOTTLING

The oven method of bottling fruit is the simplest and, although unsuitable for apples, pears, peaches and some others, it is perfectly satisfactory for small soft fruits. I use Kilner jars, which come complete with rubber sealing discs attached to the lids and separate screw bands. The jars can be used again and again but new lids must be used each time for bottling. (The old ones can be used for dry storage).

First, wash the jars in hot, soapy water, rinse thoroughly and dry in the oven.

Only fruit which is in perfect condition should be used for bottling and it should be just ripe. Pack the jars brimful with clean, washed fruit. Stand jars on a baking sheet, place a piece of kitchen foil over the tops of the open jars and put them in a slow oven (250°F/130°C — mark ½) for the times shown, while you prepare a sugar syrup*. Soft fruits can be bottled in water but sugar syrup produces a better flavour and colour.

> Blackcurrants — 1 hour 10 minutes
> Gooseberries)
> Raspberries) — 1 hour 15 minutes
> Loganberries)
> Blackberries)
> Cherries — 1 hour 20 minutes

Remove jars from the oven and set them on a wooden or towel covered surface — a cold surface such as metal or marble could cause cracking. The fruit will have shrunk below the rims of the jars — use one jar to "top up" the others and return them to the oven for a further 5 minutes. Fill to the brim with boiling syrup.

Dip the sealing discs in boiling water, then place them on top of the jars and screw down tightly. Next day, test for a proper seal by removing screw bands and lifting jars by the lids. The lids should remain firm — if not, repeat the preserving process using new lid. Label and store in a cool, dry and airy situation.

*To make 1½ pints (850 ml — 3¾ cups) sugar syrup, put 1 pint (575 ml — 2½ cups) water and 8 oz (225 gms — 1 cup) granulated sugar in a saucepan. Bring slowly to the boil to dissolve sugar completely. Boil 2 minutes. Allow approximately ½ pint (275 ml — 1¼ cups) of syrup to 1 lb (450 gms — 1 lb) fruit.

102

DEEP FREEZING

The successful storage of soft fruits is extremely simple and will be a tremendous asset in the months to come. A deep freezer will store fresh produce for up to one year. (One star on the freezing compartment of a domestic refrigerator indicates recommended storage for up to 1 week, two stars for 1 month and three stars for 3 months). Fruit pies and ice creams will keep in the deep freezer for 2-3 months.

Raspberries and **strawberries** certainly deserve as much space in the freezer as you can allow them. They should be frozen as soon as possible after picking and be in prime condition. In my opinion, both preserve their shape and texture better if frozen without the use of sugar but, if you prefer, they can be frozen in dry sugar or sugar syrup. Look the berries over carefully, hull strawberries, and discard any mouldy or blemished fruit. Pack the firm, dry fruit in polythene bags, preserving jars, wax tubs specially made for the purpose, or simply in clean punnets, wrapped in polythene. Allow at least ½" (1¼ cm) headroom in containers or punnets.

To pack in dry sugar, allow 4 oz (125 gms — ½ cup) caster sugar for 1 lb (450 gms — 1 lb) fruit. To make approximately 3 pints (1¾ litres — 7½ cups) sugar syrup, dissolve 1 lb (450 gms — 2 cups) sugar in 1 quart (1.150 litres — 5 cups) water, bring to the boil, then remove immediately from heat and allow to cool. Allow 1 pint (575 ml — 2½ cups) syrup for each 2 lbs (1 kg — 2 lbs) of fruit. Place berries in tubs or jars and cover fruit with cold syrup.

You can also "open" freeze all soft fruits, in single layers, on trays and then simply pack them in polythene bags—an excellent method.

To freeze Raspberry, Blackcurrant or Gooseberry Pies. Line your pie plate with short crust pastry. Top and tail blackcurrants or gooseberries and fill pie with fresh fruit, sweetened with 4 oz (125 gms — ½ cup) sugar to the lb (450 gms — lb). Moisten rim of pastry and press on pastry lid but do not make slits in the centre. Slip pie into a polythene bag and freeze. When frozen, remove pie from plate, wrap in greaseproof paper and store in a tin or cake box in the freezer for up to 3 months. (Label box with the date).

To bake, replace pie in pie dish, make slits in the top and bake in a hot oven (425°F/220°C — mark 7) until browned — about 50 minutes.

Pies may also be frozen after baking but this will not result in quite such a crisp crust. Cool baked pies before wrapping and freezing. To re-heat — place in a moderate oven (375°F/190°C — mark 5) for about 30 minutes.

Ice cream and frozen desserts. These will keep in the deep freezer for 2 to 3 months. Pack home-made ice creams, etc. in sealed, plastic containers (the sandwich box type is suitable). Place in ordinary refrigeration for ½ to 1 hour before serving.

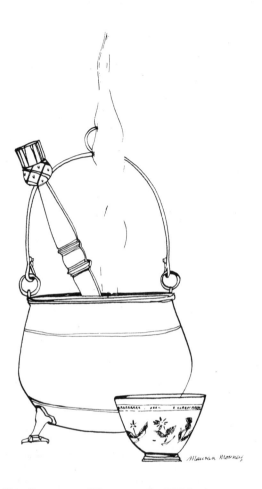

Other Good Things

This heading is necessary, if for no other reason than to accommodate the recipe for porridge, surely the staple breakfast food of any **real** Scot, even today! But it will serve also to include other good things quite unique to Scotland, such as "Tablet" (only distantly related to fudge), Athol Brose and Elderberry Wine.

"Rise up and mak' a clean fireside,
Put on the muckle pot . . ."

From an old Scots song, "There's
Nae Luck Aboot The Hoose."

CROFTER'S PORRIDGE

There is nothing like real, oatmeal porridge for breakfast — but make it, by all means, with packaged flaked oats, if you must. For each person to be served, put a good cupful (about 7/8 fl oz (225 ml — 1 cup)) of freshly run water into a saucepan and bring it to the boil, then sprinkle in a handful (2 rounded tablespoonful (2 rounded 15 ml spoons)) of oatmeal and a saltspoonful of salt, stirring continuously over reduced heat until it comes back to the boil. Let it cook very slowly for about 20 minutes, until thoroughly soft and without lumps. (If using flaked, porridge oats, it will take only 3-5 minutes).

Some say that porridge is the better for being allowed to stand and then re-heated. One Scots minister I know insists (although his wife is a first-class cook) on making the porridge himself and on making it the day before it is to be eaten. Immediately upon finishing his breakfast of porridge, he makes the porridge for the following morning.

I well remember my father at his breakfast porridge — the milk was never poured around the porridge but served in a small, separate bowl and each spoonful of porridge was dipped into this bowl of milk before being raised to his mouth. This is the old, "correct" way of eating porridge. In even older times, there was a "porridge drawer" in the crofter's kitchen dresser and, I am told, this drawer was filled with porridge which, of course, grew cold and solid in it and this was subsequently cut into squares for him to take on the hill with him, for sustenance.

There is a special, carved, wooden stick used for stirring porridge, known as a spurtle or theevil — a popular tourist trinket in gift shops — but a wooden spoon serves the purpose quite satisfactorily. Porridge should be made with water and salt only — most Scots will not even countenance adding sugar to it at table. However, being only half Scots by blood, I prefer my porridge to be made in the traditional way but scattered, in the bowl, with soft brown sugar and surrounded with creamy milk — an incomparable breakfast treat!

SWISS MILK "TABLET"

Makes about 2¾ lbs (1¼ kg)

Ingredients	Imperial	Metric	American
Fresh butter	**4 oz**	**125 gms**	**½ cup**
1 breakfastcup Milk	**8 fl oz**	**225 ml**	**1 cup**
Granulated sugar	**2 lbs**	**1 kg**	**4 cups**
1 large size tin full-cream condensed milk			

It is essential to make this in a very large saucepan as the mixture rises rapidly as it boils.

Melt the butter slowly in the milk, add sugar and stir (over very gentle heat) until sugar dissolves; add condensed milk and bring slowly to the boil; still using low heat, stir continuously until mixture turns a light caramel colour and begins to thicken. (It is impossible to say exactly how long this will take as this will depend on several factors — the thickness of your pan, the degree of cooking heat, etc. — but it should take, very roughly, 20 minutes).

Remove from heat and beat vigorously until thick. (This may take only a few seconds). Pour onto well buttered, square or oblong tins. Score the tablet into squares when cool and remove from the tins when cold.

For packing, wrap each piece in a small square of cellophane.

COCONUT ICE

Makes about 1¼ lb (450 gms)

Ingredients	Imperial	Metric	American
Granulated sugar	1 lb	450 gms	2 cups
Milk	¼ pint	125 ml	10 tbsps
Small pat of butter			
Dessicated coconut	4 oz	125 gms	1¼ cups
Few drops cochineal			

Put sugar, milk and butter into a fairly large saucepan; bring slowly to the boil and simmer over a low heat, stirring continuously, for about 7 minutes or until a little of the mixture forms a soft ball when dropped into cold water. Remove from heat, add coconut and beat vigorously for a few seconds — it will thicken very quickly so have ready a well buttered square or oblong tin. Colour half the mixture pale pink with a few drops of cochineal and quickly pour on top of the other half in the tin. Score into squares and cut when cold.

For packing, wrap in small squares of cellophane.

MRS. BETSWORTH'S TREACLE TOFFEE

Makes about 1½ lbs (657 gms — 1½ lbs).

Put into a fairly large, heavy pan —

Ingredients	Imperial	Metric	American
Soft brown sugar	12 oz	350 gms	1¾ cups
Butter	4 oz	125 gms	½ cup
Treacle	8 oz	225 gms	½ lb molasses
Water	2 tbsps	2 x 15 ml spoons	2 tbsps

Heat gently together until sugar has dissolved, then add a pinch (⅛ level tsp) (⅛ x 5 ml spoon — ⅛ tsp) cream of tartar.

Boil rapidly, stirring frequently, to 260°F/127°C or until a little of the mixture forms a hard ball when dropped into cold water.

Pour into a well buttered, shallow tin, measuring about 7½" x 11" (19 cm x 28 cm). Mark into squares with a knife when toffee begins to set and break into pieces when cold.

For gifting, wrap in cellophane or wax paper and pack in a storage jar or gift box.

Note: This toffee will keep in an airtight tin for several weeks. (Provided you hide the tin!)

MACAROON BARS

Add sifted icing sugar to mashed potato (approximately one medium sized potato to 1 lb (450 gms — 3½ cups sifted) icing sugar, beating well. Do not panic when mixture goes gooey at first — just keep right on adding icing sugar and all will be well! When thick, roll out. Cut into bars. Dip into melted chocolate and coat with toasted, dessicated coconut.

ATHOLL BROSE

First, prepare an oatmeal brose. Toast ¼ lb (125 gms — 1 cup) or so of oatmeal until lightly browned and crisped, in the oven, then mix to a thick paste with cold water. Let stand until completely cold. Press the oatmeal now through a fine, wire sieve — the liquid which drops through is the oatmeal "brose" used in the recipe. (The remaining, dryish oatmeal is fine fare for the birds).

Sweeten the oatmeal brose with heather honey (clear), using about 1 dessertspoonful (2 x 5 ml spoons — 1 dstsp) of honey to each wineglassful of brose. Stir thoroughly and pour into an empty whisky bottle. Fill up with whisky (Scotch, need I say) and shake well before serving.

TODDY

A cure for all ills, especially colds — best drunk in bed!

Into a mug or heat-proof glass, stir some whisky, sugar and lemon juice — a double measure of whisky, sugar to taste or a teaspoonful (1 x 5 ml spoon) of honey, and not too much lemon — and fill up with boiling water. Stir well and drink as hot as possible.

BREAD SAUCE

Remove crusts from 2 large slices of bread and make into soft crumbs. Put crumbs into a small saucepan, along with an onion stuck with 3 or 4 cloves, salt and pepper and about ½ pint (275 ml — 1¼ cups) milk. Bring very slowly to the boil and "infuse" over low heat or at the side of the stove for at least 20-30 minutes — more time will not impair the sauce. Before serving, remove onion and cloves, stir and adjust seasoning.

KATIE'S FRESH LEMONADE

Makes about 5½ pints (3 litres — 3½ quarts) concentrated lemonade.

Ingredients	Imperial	Metric	American
6 lemons (juice of 6, rind of 3)			
Sugar	4-4¼ lbs	2 kgs	8 cups
Tartaric acid	1 oz	25 gms	1 oz
Citric acid	2 oz	50 gms	2 oz
Boiling water	3 pints	1¾ litres	7½ cups

Use a vegetable peeler to pare rind thinly from three of the lemons. Mix rind, juice, sugar and acids in a large bowl. Pour boiling water over and stir occasionally until sugar dissolves. Cool, strain and bottle.

Use 1 part concentrated lemonade to 4 parts water or soda, including some ice cubes, if available. This concoction, tinkling in a glass jug, will add delight to any summer's day.

ELDERBERRY WINE

All wine making equipment must be scrupulously clean and rinsed in very hot water just before using. The final bottles should be dried in a low oven and corks boiled.

Ingredients	Imperial	Metric	American
Elderberries, picked when black and plump	3 lbs	1¼ kg	3 lbs
Sugar	3½ lbs	1½ kg	7 cups
Water	1 gallon	4½ litres	5 quarts
Yeast and nutrient			

Wash berries and strip them from the stalks with a fork. Put them in a large bowl or plastic bucket and crush them with a potato masher or the like. Pour over them the gallon of boiling water and let it cool to approximately 70°F/21°C before adding the yeast and nutrient, according to package instructions. Cover the bowl or bucket with muslin or a clean tea towel and tie round the rim. Untie, stir and recover once daily for three days. You will now require another large bowl or plastic bucket. Put the sugar in this and strain the wine through muslin onto the sugar and stir to dissolve. Pour into stone or dark glass "demijohn" fermenting jars (the wine tends to lose colour in clear jars) but leave the top 1/6th of the jars empty — this wine has a particularly vigorous ferment — plugging the neck with cotton wool. When fermentation has quietened, fill to the bottom of the neck of the jar and fit it with an airlock. Leave until fermentation has completely stopped, which may take as long as 5 months with this wine, then siphon off into dark bottles and cork. (Different kinds of corking gadgets are available from wine equipment shops). Leave for at least six months to mature — a year to three years, if you have the will power!

MENUS FOR SCOTTISH FESTIVALS

BURNS SUPPER

(January 25th)

Cock-a-Leekie
Herring Fillets Fried in Oatmeal
THE HAGGIS
Bashed Neeps and Tatties or Clapshot
Roast Sirloin of Aberdeen Angus Beef
Cloutie Dumpling or Scotch Trifle

ST. ANDREW'S NIGHT

(November 30th)

The same menu as for Burns Supper or —

Scotch Broth
Soused Herrings with Pickled Beets, or
Smoked Salmon Roulades
Roastit Bubblyjock with Oatmeal Stuffing
Tatties and Buttered Kale or
Pheasant Pie, with Forcemeat Balls
Drambuie Soufflé or Cranachan

HOGMANAY

(New Year's Eve)

Atholl Brose or Whisky or Ginger Wine
Shortbread, Black Bun, Oatcakes
Cheeses

INDEX

110

EGG, SAVOURY AND VEGETABLE DISHES

HOT PUDDINGS AND COLD DESSERTS

CAKES, SCONES, BISCUITS AND TEABREADS

PRESERVES

OTHER GOOD THINGS